QI GONG THERAPY

The
Chin
Art o
Healing
with
Energy

QI GONG THERAPY

The Chinese Art of Healing with Energy

Maintaining
Health, Enhancing Vitality,
and Attaining Longevity
through Qi Gong Therapy

TZU KUO SHIH

Pelanduk
Publications

Published by
Pelanduk Publications (M) Sdn. Bhd.,
24 Jalan 20/16A, 46300 Petaling Jaya,
Selangor Darul Ehsan, Malaysia.

Address all correspondence to:
Pelanduk Publications (M) Sdn. Bhd.,
P.O. Box 8265, 46785 Kelana Jaya,
Selangor Darul Ehsan, Malaysia.

Perpustakaan Negara Malaysia   Cataloguing-in-Publication Data

Tzu, Kuo Shih, 1929-
    Qi Gong therapy: the Chinese art of healing with energy/
    Tzu Kuo Shih; edited by Charles Stein
    ISBN 967-978-588-2
    1. Ch'i kung. 2. Ch'i kung—History. 3. Medicine, Chinese.
    I. Stein, Charles. II. Title.
    613.7148

Printed by Percetakan Soonly Trading

無為

無不為

气功 是 揭示人类生
命的奥秘 推进世界医
学科学 使人类获得健
康长寿的最佳途径

施祖谷

Qi Gong can reveal the mystery of life. It is the best way to further world medical science and bring health, longevity, and wisdom to human kind.

Tzu Kuo Shih

道可道
非常道

These famous words of Loazi from the Dao De Jing *are usually translated:*

> The Dao that can be spoken of
> Is not the everlasting Dao.

But for the practitioner of Qi Gong they have a special meaning. "The Dao that can be spoken of" is the ordinary Dao — the way of ordinary reality that can be grasped by the senses and understood through application and study. But there is also a Dao that cannot be seen by ordinary means. Here, the application of the senses and the studious accumulation of knowledge are of no avail. This invisible Dao can only be seen by the Qi Gong Master who, as the calligraphy on the following page expresses, "desiring nothing, understands and possesses all things."

CONTENTS

Preface

Since the mid-1980s, we in the West have seen a remarkable growth in the availability of information about the ancient Chinese energy practices known collectively as "Qi Gong (Chi Kung)." Chinese masters are teaching various forms of Qi Gong; numerous books presenting Qi Gong methods have been published; several journals dedicated to Qi Gong are in circulation, and TV documentaries have made the general public aware of its existence.

In China, systems of Qi Gong practices exist in several different traditional contexts: there is Buddhist Qi Gong, Daoist Qi Gong, Qi Gong as a Martial Art, and Medical Qi Gong. *Qi Gong Therapy, Volume One* is the first in a series of books by Master Shih dealing comprehensively with the history, theory, and methods of Medical Qi Gong.

Medical Qi Gong is an aspect of Traditional Chinese Medicine. It is often practiced in conjunction with Acupuncture, Moxibustion, Herbalism, and Massage and consists of movements, postures, and breathing methods that the patient can apply without the presence and constant supervision of a physician. Of course, a Qi Gong Master is necessary to prescribe what particular methods should be used by the patient and to give instruction and correction in their application. But generally, Qi Gong Therapy is self-therapy. Under special circumstances, a Master Qi Gong practitioner may work directly with patients by increasing, enhancing, or balancing the patient's energy with his/her own. Also, many of the effects of Qi Gong can be produced by the other Traditional Chinese medical techniques; but whenever the interests and abilities of the patient allow, Qi Gong is the preferred treatment.

Though Medical Qi Gong is practiced in a clinical context, its principles are congruent with the metaphysical principles of Daoism (Taoism) and its practices are conducive to living a life in accordance with the Dao (Tao). As is the case with the other methods of Traditional Chinese Medicine, physical health is understood as being profoundly interdependent with emotional balance, harmonious life-circumstances, and spiritual well-being. The reader should therefore not be surprised to find that most Qi Gong methods emphasize quiet meditation and that instructions involve the correction of the pateint's emotional and spiritual state as well as manipulations of the body.

Qi Gong Therapy, Volume One is an overview of the history and principles of Chinese Medical Qi Gong. It includes three essays that are used as introductory texts for Master Shih's two year, Qi Gong Therapy Training Course at The Chinese Healing Arts Center in Kingston, New York. The first essay presents a brief survey of the history of Medical Qi Gong with key quotations from the leading Qi Gong practitioners and theorists from each historical period. The second essay gives an outline of the three main categories of Qi Gong practice: exercises for regulating posture, for regulating the mind and emotions, and for regulating respiration. The third essay presents the relationship between Qi Gong practices and several topics from Chinese Medicine: the Zang/Fu organs, the meridians, the Jing (essence), Qi (energy) and Shen (spirit), the objective status of "Qi," and a brief survey of modern scientific studies regarding various aspects of Qi Gong practice.

Qi Gong Therapy, Volume Two will deal with diagnostic methods, and subsequent volumes will present specific Qi Gong techniques for the treatment of heart and cardio-vascular problems, depression, and insomnia; liver ailments; illnesses of the digestive system; respiratory problems; arthritis and diseases of the joints, bones and marrows; male reproductive problems such as impotence and prostate disease; female reproductive and menstrual ailments; illnesses of the blood and the eyes; and diseases of the face, nose, throat, and ears.

Tzu Kuo Shih, A Biography

Master Shih was born in Shanghai, China in 1929 to an aristocratic family well-established in the medical tradition. He himself represents the fifth generation of Traditional Chinese Medical Practitioners in his family. He is renowned in China as a distinguished painter and calligrapher, and his medical writings are celebrated for their literary elegance. Master Shih began his study of Chinese Medicine and meditation practice under his grandfather after the bombing of Shanghai during the Sino-Japanese War in 1939 destroyed his family's clinic and killed his father. In the hardship following these events, he contracted malaria. The only treatment available was the traditional meditation techniques his grandfather was able to teach him. He survived but was severely weakened and subject to recurrent illness.

Even after peace was restored, food was scarce and, in fact, Master Shih's entire youth was spent under conditions of physical deprivation. During bouts of illness he would practice Qi Gong under the care of his grandfather and an uncle who was also a traditional Chinese healer. When he was well enough, he attended school, but conditions there were unsanitary and overcrowded, and there was neither time nor room for Qi Gong practice. When he was nineteen, he attended a school where forty students slept in one room, three students to a bed. Under these conditions, Master Shih developed tuberculosis with bleeding from two holes in his lung. Doctors in residence at the school did not expect him to live, and he was sent home to his family.

For three months Master Shih practiced Qi Gong exercises for his lungs as well as the Microcosmic Orbit (see page 24). In this exercise, energy is circulated through the major Yin and Yang meridians in the front and back of the body, and all the meridians are opened thereby. Unable to do anything else, he practiced continuously. After three months, the bleeding in his lungs stopped, and he soon recovered fully. Master Shih has continued his Qi Gong practice to this day.

After his illness, Master Shih continued to study with his family and was eventually apprenticed to a famous Traditional Medical practitioner, Dr. Bae, to study the Traditional Chinese Medical System as well as acupuncture technique. At the same time he studied different forms of Qi Gong and Tai Chi Quan. He was also initiated in meditation practices by some of the leading masters in China, learning various secret techniques that had been carefully guarded and passed down through specific families through the ages.

Under Maoist rule in the 1950s and 1960s, the arts that Master Shih had become proficient in became even more secret as the new regime sought to eradicate much of Chinese tradition. Qi Gong was not taught openly or even spoken of. During those years, Master Shih worked as a doctor in municipal hospitals until, in the late 70s, one of the heads of the government in Beijing was stricken with cancer and was healed by a doctor who used Qi Gong methods. The practice was instantly reinstated and has from that time been permissible in China.

At this point Master Shih was asked to teach Qi Gong to other doctors in Shanghai and was allowed to hold classes for patients who were terminally ill with cancer and other diseases. He often speaks of a class of one hundred and twenty patients in which twenty-eight had different forms of cancer. After three months of practicing an exercise called "The Healing Walk," all were cured.

After the reinstatement of Qi Gong, The Qi Gong Association of Beijing was formed to study ancient healing arts and develop their application for modern society. Master Shih is a founding member of this prestigious group, composed of some of the highest officials in China: heads of the departments of Health, Education, and Physical Therapy, famous scientists, and doctors. He still serves as a consultant to this association and, in 1986, was named one of its Honorary Directors, a distinction granted to only one hundred doctors in all of China.

Since 1982, Master Shih has been living in the United States with his wife, Deying Huang, also a well-known practitioner of Traditional Chinese Medicine, and his two daughters, Wen Jing, a Tai Chi Quan Master in her own right, and Melanie. Together they direct The Chinese Healing Arts Centers in Kingston, New York and Danbury, Connectiticut where treatment is offered on an individual basis and classes are given in various forms of Qi Gong and Tai Chi Quan.

Charles Stein
with Cassia Berman

I
HISTORY OF QI GONG

題鍾馗雅趣圖

鍾馗之出唐
代斯興肇自
道子盛于伯
年技丕驅邪
浩氣彌天吾
寫鍾邑筆遠
雲煙意向梁
牧鍾培前賢首
魁碎為再作神仙
丁卯年大暑冀庵客廂

Fan Zeng, Zhong Kui's Refined Paradise (contemporary); Zhong Kui is a figure known for his ability to dispel evil.

Introduction

The Characteristics and Functions of Qi Gong

What is Qi Gong?

Qi Gong is the art of exercising the Jing (essence), Qi (energy), and Shen (spirit). The nucleus of Qi Gong is the exercise of Yi (consciousness) and Qi (vital energy). The main purpose of these exercises is to regulate the internal functions of the human body. Qi Gong does this through developing consciousness and respiration, through causing the internal Qi to manifest in awareness, and through moving and strengthening the internal Qi. The internal Qi is the Qi belonging to the human body itself. Thus, Qi Gong brings self-regulation and self-control to the vital organs.

The Characteristics of Qi Gong

- Along with exercising and controlling one's mind and body, Qi Gong influences one's physiological state and, in particular, rectifies pathological conditions. At the same time, Qi Gong brings out latent powers within the human body and enables one to make the most of them. It increases the body's ability to adapt to and defend against the outer environment.
- Qi Gong is a holistic therapy that exercises the body and mind and increases self-regulation and self-control.
- Along with regulating respiration and consciousness, Qi Gong regulates the functions of the central nervous system.
- To practice Qi Gong one must combine Xing (shape-posture), Yi (consciousness), and Qi (vital energy). To exercise "the genuine Qi" is to exercise "The Three Treasures" of the human body: Jing (essence), Qi (vital energy), and Shen (spirit), so as to relieve pain, strengthen the body's constitution, improve intelligence, and prolong life. Xing (shape), Yi (consciousness) and Qi (vital energy), also called "The Three Regulations" by the ancient Chinese,

Shennong, traditional inventor of Chinese Herbal Therapy.

3

regulate the body's constitution, consciousness, and respiration, respectively. The regulation of these three functions are the main principles of the practice of Qi Gong.

The Main Functions of Qi Gong

The functions of Qi Gong can be summarized under the following aspects:

- Disease prevention
- Disease treatment
- Strengthening the body
- Improving intelligence and prolonging life
- Manifesting latent power

"If your energy is strong, no illness can befall you"
The Yellow Emperor's Classic of Internal Medicine.

邪 之 所 湊

其 氣 必 虛

The Development of Qi Gong

Qi Gong has a very long history. According to specific historical documents, the practice of Qi Gong in China goes back at least five thousand years. If one calculates according to certain other documents, Qi Gong may well have been practiced for more than ten thousand years. Each period of Chinese history has had important Qi Gong practitioners and physcians who have left valuable texts revealing their knowledge and insight. The remainder of this chapter will introduce representative figures and their work from each period.

From Remote Antiquity to the 21st Century B.C.

Qi Gong was practiced during the earliest period in order to maintain good health. It is said that in the period of Yao and Shun, the people knew "how to promote circulation by dancing" (from *Lü Shi Chun Qiu Gu Yue Pian* ((*The Spring and Autumn Annals*, "Ancient Music")). These ancient practices involved movements that were similar to dance and that relaxed the tendons and bones in order to strengthen the body's constitution.

正 气 存 内

邪 不 可 干

From the Xia, Shang, and Zhou Dynasties Through the Qin and Han Dynasties (21st century B.C to 220 A.D.)

The time known as "The Spring and Autumn Period" and "The Warring States Period" (the main periods for the development of Chinese science and culture) was characterized by contention between some hundred different schools of thought. In the process of clarifying their distinct positions, the schools produced systematic summaries and expositions of philosophy, natural science, medicine, Qi Gong, etc. including many important monographs and documents. Several of these schools of thought, in particular the Ru (Confucian), Shi (Buddhist), Dao (Taoist) medical and martial arts schools, each developed approaches to the practice of maintaining good health with Qi Gong.

Examples of these various approaches

Guanzi: The famous statesman from the Spring and Autumn Period, Guanzi, writes in regard to maintaining good health:

> A normal person needs happiness to maintain vitality. Sorrow causes health to disappear. The heart can keep the mind quiet. One can keep quiet by internal balance.

Laozi (Lao Tzu)

This means that the keys to health are calmness of mind and heart, happy emotion, and avoidance of anger, irritability, sorrow, sadness, or too much joy. These are emotional activities that disturb health.

Laozi, Zhuangzi, and Kang Zhuangzi: The originators and spiritual leaders of Daoism, Laozi (Lao Tzu) and Zhuangzi (Chuang Tzu) write, on keeping good health:

> The Dao that can be spoken of
> Is not the everlasting Dao.
> The name that can be named
> Is not the everlasting name.
> That which has no name
> Is the origin of Heaven and Earth.
> That which has a name
> Is the Mother of all things.

Thus if one is always without desire,
One can observe indescribable marvels.
If one is always desirous
One sees merest traces.
That is why the Sage governs himself by relaxing the mind,
Reinforcing the abdomen,
Easing the will,
And strengthening the bones.

Dao De Jing— **Laozi**

Keep the mind quiet, and the posture will be straight. It should be quiet and pure. Then your body will not grow tired. If you do not waste your essence (Jing), you will prolong your life. See nothing with the eyes; hear nothing with the ears. Know nothing. Then your mind holds its inner posture, which can be maintained.

Laozi

To keep its nature, to nourish its vital energy, to suit its virtue; to integrate with the customs that are made by the world.

Zhuangzi

To blow and listen to respiration; to get rid of the stale and take in the fresh. The bear and the bird work for life.... Body pertains to heart. Heart pertains to Qi. Qi pertains to mind. Mind pertains to nothingness.

Kang Zhuangzi

These are the "Four Pertainings."

The above passages represent typical thoughts about keeping fit from Laozi, Zhuangzi and Kang Zhuangzi, and in fact they summarize these masters' experience of Qi Gong practice. Thus they emphasize that in practicing Qi Gong one must keep the mind quiet and the respiration gentle, delicate, and deep; one must keep one's spirit within and concentrate the mind in Dantian in the lower abdomen; one must combine Yi (consciousness) and Qi (vital energy); and one must combine movement with quietness, thus achieving the "Four Pertainings."

The thoughts of Zhuangzi about keeping fit are divided into two aspects: maintaining the posture of the body and keeping presence of mind. Zhuangzi suggests that one keeps the body's posture through limiting desire; one maintains presence of mind by emptiness and quietness. When the posture (body shape) and mind are not deficient, there will be longevity.

Later generations of medical thinkers were influenced by Laozi and Zhuangzi. The school of Daoist Qi Gong coming down from them holds the keys to their methods. "The listening-to-respiration method" of Zhuangzi is still a good method in practicing Qi Gong to help eliminate distracting thoughts and bring the brain to "the quiet state."

Laozi and Zhuangzi emphasized keeping one's spirit (shen) within by concentrating the mind in the Dantian, the area in the abdomen below the navel.

Kongzi, Mengzi, and Xunzi: Here are some characteristic thoughts of Kongzi (Confucius), Mengzi (Mencius) and Xunzi, representative Confucianist thinkers from the Spring and Autumn and the Warring States periods.

Kongzi (Confucius) says:

> The death of a man is not his fate. Improper sexual activities, improper food-intake, over-easiness or over-fatigue, give rise to diseases and kill him.
>
> Flex the arm and put your head on it while sleeping.

Kongzi implies here that reclining Qi Gong practices can relax one.

Mengzi says:

> I am good at nourishing my noble spirit.

Kongzi (Confucius)

Xunzi says:

> Stop: then be calm. Be calm: then be quiet. Be quiet: then be peaceful. Be peaceful: then take thought .

These statements embody some of the key points of Qi Gong. Yanhui, a student of Kongzi, presented a method of practicing Qi Gong known as "Quiet sitting." He maintains that we should "Sit in order to forget." This requires that we keep both the outside and the inside of the body relaxed and that we become extremely calm so as to achieve the empty and open state of "Self-forgetfulness." This state is a valuable experience and it supports the experiences developed in later schools of "Nourishing one's nature" and "Sitting in meditation."

Confucius as well as the Daoists emphasized Qi Gong practice for maintaining health.

Texts from The Warring States Period: *The Inscription on the Jade Belt for Promoting Qi Circulation (Xing Qi Yu Bei Ming)* found

8

among disinterred artifacts from the early years of the Warring States Period (about the fourth century B.C.), a period during which the Chinese people had developed a rich experience of Qi Gong, says:

> Regarding the promotion of Qi circulation: if it is deep, it can be stored; if it is stored, it can be extended; if it is extended, it can go downward; if it goes downward, it can be fixed; if it is fixed, it can be consolidated; if it is consolidated, it can sprout.

Recently disinterred artifacts from the Ma Wang Du Tomb in Changsha include profound Qi Gong instructional texts from the Warring States Period (4th Century B.C.)

According to the textual research and study of Guo Mo Ruo, the above quotation is a Qi Gong breathing process. It is about the condition of the circulation of "internal Qi" as understood by these ancient people.

Among the artifacts disinterred from the Ma Wang Du Tomb in Changsha, there are two other important documents about Qi Gong. One is *Inducing Exercise Chart (Dao Yin Tu)*; the other is *Method for Eliminating Food-Intake and Promoting Qi Circulation (Bi Gu Shi Qi Fa)*. According to experts who have studied these texts, they have a much richer content than the *The Inscription on the Jade Belt for Promoting Qi Circulation (Xing Qi Yu Bei Ming)*.

Also from this time is the earliest Chinese medical text containing a complete exposition of Qi Gong, *The Yellow Emperor's Classic of Internal Medicine (Huang Di Nei Jing)*:

> The people of ancient times who knew the Dao, used the concepts of Yin/Yang and methods of Qi Gong. They had proper food in-take, a well-regulated daily life, and did not overwork, so their body and mind remained healthy. They died at age one hundred.

> The pathogenic factor of wind is to be for the most part avoided. If one is calm and peaceful and thinks nothing, the genuine Qi arises. Keep essence and mind within. Then disease cannot come.

The Yellow Emperor's Classic of Internal Medicine (Nei Jing Huang Di) is the earliest comprehensive text of Chinese medicine. It presents a systematic, rich, and complex exposition of Qi Gong.

> If one raises and supports Heaven and Earth, controls Yin and Yang, breathes Jing, keeps alone and concentrates the mind, then the muscles will be relaxed. When the kidney has been diseased for a long time, the patient is asked to face south from 3 to 5 A.M., keep the mind calm, not to think about anything, to compress the Qi seven times while holding one's breath, then to extend the neck. In this way, internal Qi will flow properly....

If the twelve organs do not lose their harmony, the well-functioning main organs will bring calmness to the lower organs. This method is for keeping fit and prolonging life.

The four seasons and Yin Yang are the bases of all things. So the wise man nourishes Yang in spring and summer and nourishes Yin in autumn and winter. Working on these bases is the gate through which all things ascend and descend, live and grow.

The wise man nourishes his body and keeps fit according to the four seasons to accommodate heat and cold; he harmonizes joy and anger to lead an easy life; he regulates Yin Yang to adjust the hard and the soft.

These thoughts about keeping fit from the *Nei Jing* originate with Laozi and Zhuangzi but go beyond them. The *Nei Jing* emphasizes accommodating oneself to nature, remaking nature, and controlling nature. It puts forward a set of methods for keeping fit that involves accommodating oneself to the changes of the four seasons and the weather. It also emphasizes practices involving not only posture, but also mind. When posture and mind are combined, longevity will follow.

Other Qi Gong Practitioners and Physicians from the Warring States Period and the Han Dynasty

Bianque was a great folk doctor during the Warring States Period who was proficient in internal medicine, surgery, gynecology, pediatrics, acupuncture, massage, Qi Gong and other methods. He conducted deep research in Qi Gong for keeping fit and also used Qi Gong as a method of diagnosis.

Quyuan was a great statesman and poet who gave a special exposition of Qi Gong in his poem *Wandering Far Away (Yuan You)* from the collection *Chu Ci*.

Zhang Zhong-Jing, an outstanding doctor of the Han Dynasty, studied Qi Gong for fitness. In his medical works, *Brief Summary of Jin Kui (Jin Kui Yao Lue)* and *Essay on Disease due to Cold and other Miscellaneous Diseases,* he discussed the zang-fu organs and the meridians. His classification of six meridians in relation to epidemic febrile disease derived from his own experience in practicing Qi Gong.

10

Wang Chong, the great philosopher and Qi Gong practitioner, thought that Qi is the source of all things and that man is transformed by material Qi. He discussed the relationship between spirit and body. His representative work, *Essay on Balance (Lun Heng)*, explains that the life of human beings is related to their congenital Qi—the hereditary quality that exists during life in relationship to acquired, environmental, and social factors. He writes:

> The longness or shortness of the life of a human is related to sufficiency or deficiency of Qi. If the Qi of the human body is sufficient and strong, life is long; if it is deficient and weak, life is short.

He also says:

> If you nourish Qi and keep it inside, then you can disperse it at the proper time. If you practice with your eyes and ears closed, keep essence within, and take medicine as a tonic at the proper time, then you can increase the production of Qi .... Life will be longer and you will never experience old age.

The philosopher Wang Chong explained that the quality of one's life is related to Congenital (Yuan) Qi, the hereditary aspect of energy.

Hua Tuo was an outstanding surgeon in the latter part of the Eastern Han Dynasty. He contributed greatly to the development of Traditional Chinese Medicine. He was also proficient in internal medicine and Qi Gong. He instructed his students to partake in physical training to benefit their health. That is the meaning of the saying, "Running water is never stale, and a door-hinge never gets worm-eaten." Accordingly he developed "Imitation of Five Animals Boxing," founded upon his own realization of the essence of Qi Gong. One of his students lived for an exceedingly long time because he persisted in practicing these forms, and he himself could still hear and see well and his teeth were still firm when he was ninety.

Hua Tuo of the Eastern Han Dynasty developed "Imitation of Five Animals Boxing," a precursor of Tai Chi Quan.

Wei Boyang was a famous chemist in the Han Dynasty and at the same time a specialist of the Taoist school in the Qi Gong of preserving health. In his famous book, *Commentary on the Book of Changes (Can Tong Qi)* he describes the main points and methods of Qi Gong practice.

11

Wei, Jin, and Northern and Southern Dynasties (220-581 A.D.)

During this period, Traditional Chinese Medicine and methods for preserving health through Qi Gong developed rapidly. Representative figures and typical works for this period include:

Ge Hong: A great medical worker and a specialist in Daoist Qi Gong for preserving health during the Jin dynasty, Ge Hong wrote *Bao Puzi's Inner Treatise*, which produced a great impact on the development of Qi Gong in later ages. He wrote:

> The movement of everything depends on Qi . It is most important that we treasure the essence of life and maintain the normal circulation of Qi.

He suggested that in breathing exercises, it is of no importance which animal you imitate. You can stretch or bend your body, bow or elevate your head, lie or walk, pace up and down or walk slowly. You can chant or breathe naturally. All these are possible movements for physical and breathing exercises. When you do the exercises you should control your breath and use the airflow to dredge the channel system of the body. In this way, Doing breathing and physical exercises can prevent the attack of diseases and regulate disordered flow of Qi and blood. Only thus can Qi circulate throughout the body fluently. If you do not exercise, stagnancy of Qi and stasis of blood will occur.

Ge Hong also said:

> A person who is good at controlling his circulation of Qi can be in good psychosomatic training within and defend against external disease-causing factors. Exploiting the Dao of preserving health, one circulates one's Qi day and night with persistence. Thus one is far from sickness.

Tao Hongjing: He was an eminent herbalist and specialist in health-preserving Qi Gong during the Northern and Southern Dynasties. Among his works are *The Atlas of Physical, Breathing, and Health-Preserving Exercises (Yang Shen Dao Ying Tu)* and *How to Preserve Your Health and Extend Your Life (Yang Shan Yen Ming Lu)*. These works summarize many ancient methods for preserving health. In addition Tao Hongjing put forward his own views, which influenced to some extend the development of Qi Gong in later times. He wrote that the main points of preserving health are that we must treasure our vitality and not dissipate Qi, and that we must pay attention to the adjustment of posture, physical breathing and movements, speech, diet, and sexual life. He held that if you want to regulate Qi to treat disease, you must control your mental activities and concentrate Qi upon the local region where the disease occurs. For example, if you have a headache, you regulate Qi and concentrate it on the head. The symptom will be relieved and the disease cured. He said:

Tao Hongjing, an herbalist of the Northern and Southern Dynasties, recommended controlling mental activities and concentrating Qi upon parts of the body where disease occurs.

> The general principle is that those who always remain calm and patient will have a long life span and those who are always irritable will have a short life span. However, if the patient person doesn't know how to preserve his health with proper practices, he will die early, and if the irritable person does know how to preserve his health, he will have an extensive lifespan.

He instructed that you should inhale with your nose and exhale with your mouth. There is one type of inhalation and six healing sounds. If patients practice Qi Gong seriously using these types of breathing, they will get good results, disease will be cured, and their lifespan will be extended.

The Classic of Abdominal Breathing is a famous ancient work on Qi Gong. The writer was a Daoist. It is said that this book was published before the Sui and Tang Dynasties. It is a monograph with commentaries on abdominal breathing (navel breathing) in Qi Gong exercises. According to this work:

> If you understand the law of the regulation of mind and Qi, you can concentrate Qi in the lower abdomen and control the circulation of Qi by means of the mind. If you integrate mind and Qi as a unit, you can prolong your life.

The Classic of the Yellow Court (Huang Ting Jing) was produced by **Mrs. Hua Cun** during the Eastern Jin Dynasty. It is an important document of the Mao Shan division of the Daoist school. It summarized the experiences in Qi Gong health-preserving methods of its predecessors and put forward many foundational theories and concrete methods of Qi Gong that would survive into later times. It has been praised by specialists in Qi Gong in the Daoist School and honored with the title of "The Best Classic for Extended Lifespan."

If you integrate mind and Qi as a unit, you can prolong your life.

13

Sui, Tang, and Five Dynasties Period (581-979 A.D.)

Health-Preserving Qi Gong developed rapidly during this period. Here are some of the most influential figures and their works:

General Treatise on the Etiology and Symptomatology of Diseases (Zhu Bing Yuan Hou Lun): In this work by **Cao Yuanfang** of the Sui Dynasty, there are many descriptions of physical and breathing exercises. Cao instructed that the patient lie on his back and take off his clothes gently and slowly. One should make use of a pillow 10 cm high, make a fist and extend one's arms, control one's mind, keep calm, regulate one's breath and eliminate distracting thoughts. Concentrate on the regulation of Qi.

General Treastise on the Etiology of Disease by Cao Yuanfang of the Sui Dynasty, gathers together many physical and breathing exercises.

Zhi Yi was a monk who also at this time spread an exercise method called "Zhi Guan Fa" which he had developed based on a summary of the methods of sitting meditation and the prolonged and intense contemplation of the Buddhists. He described the training method regarding posture, breath, and mind-regulation and put forward the "Six Steps" conducive to mind regulation.

Sun Simiao was a renowned physician and Daoist of the Tang Dynasty. There are many descriptions of Qi Gong practices in his works, *Essential Prescriptions Worth a Thousand in Gold (Qian Jin Fang)* and *Supplement to the Prescriptions Worth a Thousand in Gold (Qian Jin Yi Fang)*. In the chapter, "Methods of Breath-Regulation" he details four methods: abdominal breathing, internal seeing, breath-controlling, and exhalation. The four methods are the essence of ancient Chinese Qi Gong.

In the work of Sun Simiao, a renowned Daoist physician of the Tang Dynasty, breathing methods became highly specialized.

In his *Song for Eliminating Diseases in the Four Seasons (Si Ji Qu Bing Ge)*, Dr. Sun wrote:

> Exhaling with mouth not open can improve the sight and soothe the liver in spring. Exhaling with the mouth open wide, in spring, can clear away the heart-fire. Exhaling with the mouth open but teeth clenched in autumn, can astringe the lung and relieve cough and asthma. Exhaling can reinforce the kidney. Producing the sound "shee—" can eliminate restlessness and fever of deficiency type of San-jiao. Rapid exhalation can reinforce the spleen and promote digestion.

14

In *The Song For Eliminating Diseases By Sun Zheng Ren (Sun Zheng Ren Wei Shen Ge)* Dr. Sun asked people to comb their hair frequently, do breathing exercises, knock their teeth together gently, swallow their saliva, and massage their face with their hands. He also said people should take a walk and stroke their abdomen after each meal.

Dr. Sun emphasized the importance of the exclusion of the seven emotions in preserving health. He pointed out that

> preserving health is not complicated. To live in accordance with the Dao means not being over-concerned about good food or bad, whether one wins or loses, attains honor or humiliation, whether one is a master or a servant, and not to have too much sexual desire. Rather one should keep calm and not over-exert oneself, keep in shape and not over-work. If you combine producing Qi and promoting its circulation continuously, you will have longevity. An ordinary person cannot very well avoid thinking—but he can learn to reduce it gradually.

The keys to Qi Gong exercise and keeping fit expounded by Dr. Sun conform to scientific laws and are quite feasible. They influence later theories about Qi Gong and preserving health. According to modern scholarship, Sun Simiao lived to be one hundred and two. His longevity is surely related to his practice of Qi Gong.

Wang Shou was another famous Qi Gong practitioner from the Tang Dynasty. In his work, *The Medical Secrets of an Official (Wai Tai Mi Yao)*, he says:

Daoist Immortal Li T'ieh-kuai by Yen Hui, 14th Century

> The method to treat diseases of the heart and abdomen and all other diseases is through breathing.

Sima Cheng-Zhen was a well-trained Qi Gong practitioner and Daoist from the Tang Dynasty who wrote, *The Book of Keeping Fit by a Hermit (Tian Yin Shi Yang Shen Shu), On Sitting and Forgetting (Zuo Wang Lun)*, and other classics on Qi Gong and keeping fit, that influenced later Qi Gong theories. He thought that there are five steps or stages to practicing Qi Gong:

1. Abstaining from meat, wine, etc. (emphasizing the relation between bodily exercise and nutrition);
2. Finding a quiet place to practice Qi Gong;

Sima Cheng-Zhen of
the Tang Dynasty
thought that the
development of Qi
Gong leads to the
magical control of
Yin/Yang and the
attainment of
cosmological insight.

3. Storing and thinking (to store the mind; to think about the body): close the eyes and concentrate the mind. If you want to return to the source of life, the key is to be quiet and watch inside;

4. Sitting and forgetting (to forget both you and me, forget heaven, earth, and things);

5. Explaining the mind. (All things are controlled by magic: in the final stage of practicing Qi Gong, one can control yin and yang, can know the ever-lasting universe and realize why it should be.)

He also organized these ideas into the "Four Explanations":

xin (abstaining from meat, wine, etc.),
xian (a quiet place),
hui (storing and thinking,
ding (sitting and forgetting).

These are also called the Four Gates. The Four Gates explain the mind magically. Sima Cheng-Zheng explains in his book, *On Inducing Qi (Dao Yin Lun)*:

> The inducing Qi exercise is to be practiced from 3 a.m. to 5 a.m. on a day with fair weather. Face the east, sit quietly without moving. Close your eyes and concentrate the mind. Knock your teeth together three hundred and sixty times so as to induce Qi and promote Qi circulation up and down.

Lü Dong-Bin was a
highly influential
Daoist of the Tang
Dynasty.

Lü Dong-Bin. He was the foremost Daoist Qi Gong practitioner of the Tang Dynasty who wrote *One Hundred Word Tombstone (Bai Zi Bei)*. This text consists of twenty sentences totaling one hundred words, describing in detail Qi Gong methods and keys to practice. It became very influential in later times.

Lü Dong-Bin writes:

> Develop Qi and forget about speaking. Calm the mind and do not move. Every movement must have its motive and resource. Do nothing without a reason.

Li Bai, Du Fu, and Bai Ju-yi: These great poets of the Tang Dynasty were also Qi Gong researchers. In their poems there are descriptions of Qi Gong practices. For example, in a poem of Bai Ju-yi there are the lines:

Close eyes and sit quietly.
Harmonize Qi-circulation and renew the muscles.
Externally, the hundred bones are relaxed.
Keep no distracting thoughts within.
Be carefree and forget that you exist.
Make the heart empty.

These words describe the comfortable state wherein one is totally quiet.

In this period, because of cultural and scientific exchanges between China and other Asian countries, the medical practices and theories of Qi Gong began to spread. In the Sui and Tang Dynasties, Indian medicine and fitness practices (Yoga) as well as massage were brought into China along with Buddhism and Buddhist methods for keeping fit and preserving health.

Li Bai (Li Po)

Song Jing Yuan (A.D. 960-1368)

During this period, Qi Gong in relation to recuperation was further developed. Major works of the Northern Song Dynasty include *Su Shen Excellent Prescription* by the literary figure **Su Shi** and the scientist **Shen Kuo**. In this work it is written that

> after midnight every day, one should sit cross-legged with one's coat on facing south or east; one should move one's teeth up and down 36 times while making a fist with each hand, holding one's breath, and looking inward to the internal organs of the body. One should visualize that the lung is white, the liver green, the spleen yellow, the heart red, and the kidneys black. Then one should think that the heart is a scorching fire, visualizing its light clearly radiating down into the pubic region. One should wait for the abdomen to fill with breath and then expel the breath slowly. One should wait for breathing to become even and rotate the tongue between the lips and teeth. Then one should rinse one's mouth with saliva and swallow it. One should practice altogether nine breath-holdings and three rinses.

During the Song Jing Yuan periods, the use of Qi Gong for recuperation from illness was greatly developed.

It is also mentioned in this work that one should hold one's breath very often and practice until one can make five throbs of one's pulse equal one breath. It was also suggested that eating lightly at supper and leaving some room in the stomach will help the circulation of the breath. If one has time when there is nothing

In the work of Su Shi and Shen Kuo, the discovery of the relationship between internally visualized colors and the health of the organs was increasingly applied.

17

to do during the day, one should close one's eyes, look inward from time to time, swallow one's saliva, and rub one's ears and eyes. In order to develop the true breath one must be quiet and completely concentrated.

During the Song period, the Daoist **Zhang Zi Yang** wrote *Understanding Truth (Wu Zheng Pian)* about Qi Gong and recuperation. During this period the Daoists were divided into southern, northern, eastern, and western groups. Zhang was the head of the southern group. The northern group, best known for its seven renowned Daoists, was headed by **Wang Chong Yang**; the eastern group was headed by **Lu Qian Yang** who wrote the book, *Unofficial History of Fang Hu (Fang Hu Wai Shi)*; and the western group was headed by **Li Han Xu** who wrote *Nine Levels of Training The Heart/Mind (Jiu Ceng Lian Xin)*. These groups were divided according to the different places in the body on which they recommended that one should concentrate when practicing Qi Gong.

In the Southern Song Dynasty, the patriotic poet **Lu You** was knowledgeable about Qi Gong. In his books *Summer Time (Xia Ri)* and *Works After Sickness (Bing Hou Zuo)*, he discusses his experience of recuperation. He writes:

> If one gazes along the edge of one's nose silently, vital energy will appear. One's two eyes can see through the night, combing white hair in the morning.

He also wrote:

> Illuminated by the heart's shine, flowing with silence is the mighty and unbroken breath from the heels.

Zhang Yun Fang wrote *Seven Essays of Yun Ji (Yun Ji Qi Jian)*, a Qi Gong monograph of the Daoist school. He stated in the book that he relied on his heart, using vital energy which would fit his body and cure disease. This is using the method of thinking to cure diseases. According to Zhang Yun Fang there are four ways of curing:

1. using the breath and thinking of light to attack the disease;
2. using the breath and thinking of the five internal organs to attack disease;
3. thinking of fire to burn out the disease;

4. thinking of taking a bath of milk to attack the disease.

In the Song period, **Chen Zhi** wrote *Providing for the Aged*. He had many experiences with Qi Gong that are worth noticing.

> To live a long life, the only efficient way is to look after one's health. The first method is to reduce one's speaking in order to keep one's internal energy. The second method is to overcome the urge for sex in order to keep essential energy (Jing). The third is to eat less heavy food in order to keep blood-energy. The fourth is to swallow one's saliva in order to help the viscera. The fifth method is to refrain from getting angry easily, in order to preserve liver-energy. The sixth is to prepare one's food well in order to preserve the stomach. The seventh is not to be obsessed with thoughts, in order to preserve the heart-energy.

> Every person relies on energy. Energy is supported by the spirit. Keeping energy means to obtain spirit. Keeping energy can be regarded as the fundamental principle.

Every person relies on energy (Qi). Qi is supported by spirit (shen).

It was also said that

> if one suffers from a certain disease and one is aware in one's heart, one can cure it with one's heart. When one feels quiet at heart, one can quiet the rest of the body. The mind is the commander of the body. The vital energy nourishes the Qi. Improving one's Qi increases one's vitality. Improving one's food improves one's Qi.

If one suffers disease and one is aware in one's heart (Xin), one can cure that disease with one's heart.

Food is important for people. That is to say, eating well can cause one's energy to be healthy. Food can increase energy to a high degree. This is the meaning of the fact that the spleen and stomach are very important organs.

The so-called four great Confucianists of the Song and Min periods all knew a great deal about Qi Gong and recuperation. What they stressed was to practice silent Gong Fu. The main method was to sit calmly.

The so-called four great medical scientists, **Liu Yuan Su, Zhang Chong Zhen, Li Guo,** and **Zhu Zhen Xiang,** were all great experts in Qi Gong and recuperation. In the book, *Essay on Preserving Life (She Shen Lun)*, Liu Yuan Su empasized a way of exercisizing for vigour, energy, and spirit, using internal visualization,

Qi-induction, and Saliva-swallowing, adjusting one's breathing, guarding one's energy, and exchanging breath in a way that irrigates the internal organs and balances the yin and yang.

Zhang Chong Zhen, in his book, *Self-Practice in the Confucian Tradition (Ru Men Shi Qin)*, mentions a Qi Gong practice that involves using thought and blowing air to cure disease.

Li Guo pointed out in his book, *Ten Books of Dong Heng (Dong Heng Shi Qin)* that those who experience an excess of joy or those who are angry, worried or frightened, ruin their vitality. He considered Qi to be the root both of spirit (Shen) and essence (Jing). If a person stores up energy (Qi), it will become Jing (essence). Stored up Qi together with Jing will become Shen (spirit). If one wants to have Shen, one must have quiet. One who masters this method can become an excellent person.

Li Dong Heng had repeatedly stressed the importance of maintaining the spleen and the stomach. He thought that a person's vitality comes from these organs and that vitality is the root of spirit. Storing up vitality will result in vigour, and storing up vigour will result in the manifestation of Shen. Therefore the vitality of the spleen and stomach is the basis of a person's life. His advice regarding recuperation from illness is to diminish the intake of food, diminish sexual activity, speak less, and reduce physical labor. These practices also constitute an effective way to assure the vitality of the spleen and stomach. A person who is full of vitality can live a long time.

Zhu Dan Xi mentions in his book, *Essay of Ge Zhi Yu (Ge Zhi Yu Lun)*, that one must adjust oneself in order to fit the four seasons. One should adjust one's breath and posture often. This can be taken as the principle behind curing disease. If one's health is not strong enough one can use energy to strengthen it. If one is hurt because of overwork, one will lose energy, thus losing strength. Only when one's energy is restored can one's health be regained. Zhu Dian Xi also wrote that what is responsible for storage in the body is the kidneys. What is responsible for excretion is the liver. The functions of these two organs are contradictory, but they are controlled by the brain. He stressed the function of adjustment between the heart's fire and the kidney's water. He thought that the heart fire and the kidney water should rise and

Chu Chi-i, Pines and Cranes, Daoist Symbols of Long Life, 1740

Zhu Dan Xi of the Yuan period wrote that one must adjust oneself internally according to the four seasons.

fall reciprocally and in this way help each other. If one wants to mend the heart, one must mend the kidneys. If one wants to mend the kidneys, one must obtain quiet in one's heart. This insight is of great importance for later developments in Qi Gong recuperative theory.

Another influential author in the Yuan period was **Chen Xu Bai,** the author of *Guide to the Gui Zhuang Point (Gui Zhong Zhi Nan).*

Min Qin Period (A.D. 1368-1840)

During this period medical science and Qi Gong developed very rapidly. The representative figures and their works are as follows:

Gong Ju Zhong: He was a doctor in the Imperial hospital during the Min Dynasty. He was also a Qi Gong expert and he introduced skills for curing disease and attaining long life. Among the skills he introduced are:

1. eliminating indigestion by special breathing techniques;
2. curing toothache by knocking the teeth together;
3. curing eye disease by moving the eyes;
4. getting rid of headache by rubbing the ear;
5. rubbing the abdomen to make stagnant Qi flow.

During the Min dynasty, Qi Gong methods grew in specificity in technique.

In the books, *Removing Pain (Qu Bing Mi Jue)* and *Silent Sitting (Jing Zuo Gong Fu),* he emphasized the importance of paying attention to the Dantian in practicing Qi Gong. Qi Gong practice should be understood as intended to exercise the breath and regulate the Shen. He pointed out that the Dantian is the place from which the Qi is regulated. It is just like a plant getting energy from its stem and root. The rising and descending of the Qi has the Dantian as its root. If the root is pulled up, water and fire can't move up and down. When the heart fire is blazing too strongly and the kidney water is dried up, a hundred illnesses appear. But there are many ways to remove the disease and make life long: one can practice by walking, sitting, standing, or lying on a bed. If one keeps on practicing every day, in ten days the blood will flow in good order and not be disturbed. The spirit will be stable and never waver, the sick person will recover and

The Dantian is the place from which the Qi is regulated.

his tired-out body will become a healthy one once more; his pale complexion will improve. Suddenly one will feel that vigour is awakening in one's marrow. Keeping energy will cause the genitals to grow strong, the eyes to brighten and piles to disappear. All disease will be eliminated. These practices are simple but have a powerful effect. This is regarded as the principle of keeping fit and the secret of defending against disease.

Li Ting: He was a famous doctor and expert in Qi Gong during the Min Dynasty. In his book, *Recuperation in Medical Science (Yi Xue Ru Men Bao Yang Shuo)*, he introduced several Qi Gong practices and principles:

1. keeping the mind inside the body to make the body calm;
2. the mind controls the breath, and the breath follows the mind; when these are working together, the Shen will be strong and problems will disappear;
3. the blood is produced by energy, energy supported by Shen.

Shou-lao, god of longevity, late 18th Century

Len Qian: He practiced Qi Gong in the Min Dynasty and wrote *Principles of Practice (Xiu Lin Yao Zhi)* in which he included *Keeping Balance During the Four Seasons (Si Shi Tiao She)*. He also included *The Song of Curing Disease (Si Ji Que Bing Ge)*, *Sixteen Words for Acquiring Longevity (Chang Sheng Shi Liu Zi Jue)*, *Guarding sounds (Dao Yin Ge Jue)* and other works. He comprehensively summed up the experience of the ancients and expressed them in his own words. What he stated in his work was simple and practical and he had a certain influence on later Qi Gong experts. For example, he pointed out in *Sixteen Words for Acquiring Longevity* that if one sits up straight with eyes closed while making a fist and calming the heart, touching the tongue to the upper palette, stirring the saliva in the mouth and swishing it 36 times, then swallowing and letting the saliva flow down to the Dantian, all diseases will go away. In his works he combined his own experience with the experiences of the entire tradition.

Gong Yan Xian was a doctor of the Imperial hospital during the Min Dynasty. He wrote *Living a Long Life and Preserving Fundamental Energy (Shou Shi Bao Yuan)* which discoursed upon breathing and standing Qi Gong. He wrote:

It is said a person's life is based on energy. When the

22

breath occurs between the heart and the spleen, then the blood flows smoothly, the vitality is strengthened, and all diseases disappear. At midnight, noon, dawn, and dusk, stay in your room quietly, the bed fitted with a heavy cotton-padded mattress, and sit on the bed with legs crossed, closing your eyes and filling your ears with cotton, not thinking anything—take your breath between your heart and spleen, not too fast and not too slow. Just take it easy. When you practice this for two months you will get Qi Gong results.

Gao Lian: He was a famous expert in Qi Gong during the Min Dynasty. He wrote *Living a Long Life and How to Cure Disease (Yan Nian Que Bing Zhai)* in which he summed up the experience of ancient Qi Gong practitioners. He invented a way of maintaining the heart, lung, and spleen.

Li Shi Zhen was a great medical scientist during the Min Dynasty. In *Examination of the Eight Secondary Channels and Other Matters (Ji Jing Ba Mai Kao)*, he wrote about the relationship between Qi Gong and the collateral channels. He pointed out that the network inside of the body can only be examined by looking within. Only those who practice Qi Gong very well can have the experience of vital energy flowing in this inner network.

Li Shi Zhen of the Min Dynasty developed the relationship between Qi Gong and the collateral channels—the eight special channels that exist in addition to the meridians associated with the Zang-fu organs.

Qu Xian Ji wrote two books, one called *The Book of Hidden Consciousness (Shen Yin Shu)* and the other, *The Inner Method of Preserving Life (Huo Ren Xin Fa)*. He introduced a way of practicing Qi Gong that stressed keeping the spirit. He wrote:

> Each person who conserves his health has his own method. In brief, the idea is not to spoil the Jing, damage the Qi, or hurt the Shen. One should get up when the cock crows, sit on one's bed and adjust the breath, moving the teeth and concentrating attention for some time. As soon as one has settled down, one should circulate energy through the microcosmic orbit ten times. The Qi should pass throughout the whole body each time. Then one will feel the blood pulsing through the whole body. At that time, saliva is produced and a happy and radiant expression appears on the face. One should then swallow the saliva, which will benefit health. Furthermore, one should sit with eyes closed, making a fist in order to become calm,

and move one's teeth up and down 36 times holding one's head in one's hands.

All these books greatly influenced the development of later Qi Gong.

Xu Ling Tai was a famous doctor during the Qing Dynasty. He wrote *The Source of Medicine (Yi Xue Yuan Lun)*. According to Xu Lin Tai, the length of a person's life depends on his vitality and on the principle of recuperation. The doctor's prescription also depends on vitality.

Wang Ang was a famous doctor and expert in Qi Gong. He summed up the ancients' experience and, on the basis of his own experience, wrote *The Great Book of Using Medicine (Wu Yao Yuan Quan)*.

From the above it can be seen that Qi Gong has a long history. It originated during the Stone Age about ten thousand years ago and has been mentioned in written documents for at least five thousand years. It was practiced by a vast number of different people. During its long development it has always been involved with people's health. It contains very efficient methods appropriate for the regulation of people's lives. In the present period we must study Qi Gong scientifically. We must discover the marrow of Qi Gong—what it is that really benefits people's health and results in long life.

At present, the study of Qi Gong both in China and in other countries is developing rapidly. Qi Gong is not only being used to guard against particular diseases, but to improve the quality of health. It also promises to yield results of interest in other fields of scientific study. One can predict that studying Qi Gong may reveal the secret of human life and make great contributions to the development of the scientific study of the nature of life in general. This can help advance medical science and other sciences throughout the world.

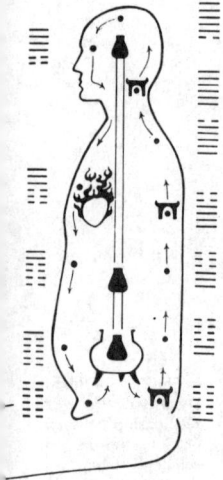

Diagram shows energy centers on the Microcosmic Orbit and their corresponding I-Ching Hexagrams

In the Microcosmic Orbit exercise, Qi energy is circulated around the Du and Ren channels. Qi is made to pass around the front and back of the body and the major centers along these paths are opened.

II

THE THREE MAIN METHODS
OF QI GONG

Chao Meng-fu, Twin
Pines Against a Flat
Vista, *ca. 1310.*

The Three Methods

It is necessary for the trainee in Qi Gong to master three groups of exercises and the principles governing them: 1. exercises for regulating the body; 2. exercises for regulating the heart/mind (Xin); 3. exercises for regulating respiration. We will discuss these three groups and the principles associated with each.

1. Regulating the Body

(BODY POSITIONS IN QI GONG)

The Significance of Regulating The Body

Regulating the body means keeping the body in the correct posture while exercising. Correct posture helps relax the body and brings about a state of inner quiet. It also helps regulate and circulate Qi, thus creating a basis for regulating the respiration and the heart/mind (Xin). If the body is in an incorrect posture, the Qi will be obstructed or damaged. Obstructed or damaged Qi will result in restlessness of mind, while restlessness of mind will further disturb the Qi. Correct posture is thus a very important part of Qi Gong exercise.

If the body is in an incorrect posture, the Qi will be obstructed or damaged.

There have been thousands of exercise schools and methods since ancient times, but they have all employed the same five or six basic postures, i.e., walking, standing, sitting, lying, kneeling etc. Different postures have different functions. They variously affect muscular tension, the burden of weight on the different regions of the body, and the circulation and reassignment of blood. They also influence the circulation of vital energy as well as the general functional activity of the Zang Fu organs and the meridians.

Different postures have different functions.

Basic Postures for Regulating the Body

1. *Walking.* There are various Qi Gong walking exercises in which the trainee learns to "walk like the wind."

2. *Standing.* Exercises performed while standing exist for various standing postures: upright, equal footing, squatting, horse-stance, "A" or "V" stance. In all standing postures, weight is delivered clearly to the ground through the feet. The body must

stand steadily like a pine tree or like a living plant. Standing exercises are accompanied by a variety of hand positions, the most important of which include: two hands hanging down naturally by the sides; hands holding an imaginary ball; crossed hands; hands pressing downward; the "five hearts facing upward" position (involving the two palms, two soles of feet, and the heart); closing palms; holding fist; crossing hands naturally and placing them on the abdominal Dantian.

Both walking and standing postures exercise the skeletal muscles and induce Qi to descend quickly. This helps strengthen the body's constitution and is good for patients whose syndromes involve excess in the upper body and deficiency in the lower body.

3. *Sitting.* There are various sitting positions, such as sitting on a chair, sitting cross-legged on the floor, sitting with back supported, etc. In all positions, the body must be stable. Stable sitting has been called "sitting like a block." The sitting positions help the practitioner relax and get into a quiet state and also are conducive to collecting vital energy in the Dantian.

4. *Lying.* There are various prone positions, such as lying face down and lying on one's side. While lying on one's side, the practitioner must "lie like a bow." For practicing "abdominal respiration," increasing gastrointestinal activity, and improving digestion and absorption, the lying position is superior to walking, standing, or sitting.

Lying and sitting are both recommended for relaxing the skeleton and the muscles, restraining the mind and encouraging inner quiet, and regulating the function of the central nervous system.

In all the positions, the practitioner must maintain a steady relationship to gravity during exercise, and the whole body must be natural, comfortable, and relaxed. In general, the practitioner should allow the whole body to be as relaxed as possible.

The specific requirements for sitting and standing positions are as follows:

- Keep nothing in mind
- Straighten the back
- Lower the shoulders and elbows
- Relax the lumbus and hip

- Keep the armpits loose
- Keep the head in a straight position
- Slightly close the eyelids
- Keep the chin slightly tucked in towards the neck
- Let the gaze be (down) along the nose
- Align the nose with the navel

Choice of Position in Qi Gong Exercise

The selection of an appropriate position is made on the basis of the characteristics of the individual's body, the disease that is being treated, and the length of time being devoted to the exercise. The following are general recommendations often given for various types of disorders. Patients suffering from hypertension, heart disease, or neurosis are first given a sitting position and later a combination of sitting and standing. This helps to move the Qi and blood downward. Patients with gastrointestinal disease begin by lying on the back or on the right side and later combine sitting with lying in order to promote gastrointestinal peristalsis, digestion, and absorption. For patients with gastroptosis, digestive dysfunction, or prolapse of the internal organs, it is correct to select lying on the back with buttocks slightly raised (lifting the hips approximately 30 cm). Patients with chronic bronchitis, asthma, emphysema, or cardiac pulmonary functional deficiency may apply a semi-reclining position (with back leaning against the wall). This helps keep respiration smooth and alleviates the symptoms of palpitation and shortness of breath. For senile or feeble patients or patients with very severe symptoms, it is incorrect to use a standing position, but rather sitting or lying down is recommended. When the patient's condition has improved somewhat, a standing position may be applied. Generally speaking, the sitting position is correct for most patients. Therefore, the sitting position is the most common posture used in Qi Gong.

To sum up, the exercise position should be chosen according to disease and individual constitution. Don't force everyone to use the same position. At the same time, it is not a good idea to change positions too frequently even after a patient has learned to use a posture and has practiced in it for some time. Generally,

Wang Shing-min, After Chu-jan's Snow Scene, *17th Century*

the beginner should choose one or two positions—a main position and a secondary position. If a standing position is selected as the primary position at the beginning, the sitting position can be added as the secondary. If the standing position is used in the morning, sitting might be used in the afternoon or evening. If the exercise period is for an hour or more, the trainee may choose to stand for the first half-hour and sit for the remainder of the period. Alternating exercise positions in this way will prevent fatigue and quicken the speed with which the exercise will take affect.

> It is not a good idea to change positions too frequently.

The Essential Factor In Regulating The Body—Relaxation

Why the Body Needs Relaxation

We all know that living in society, the body is involved in intense work or study every day. Even children, though exempt from labor, are involved in mental activity and encounter various stimulations from internal and external environmental factors, causing tension and unhappiness. Most people dream when they are asleep, indicating that even in sleep the brain is not fully at rest. All these factors often result in tensions of various kinds affecting muscles, nerves, vessels and viscera, resulting, in turn, in abnormal bodily conditions. Qi Gong methods are therefore designed to help the muscles, vessels, nerves, etc., of the whole body relax. Relaxation helps the circulation of Qi and blood and improves the coordination of the activity of the brain with all the viscera. It is also advantageous for metabolism, as well as for the collection, storage, and circulation of Zheng Qi (anti-pathogenic Qi).

> Relaxation helps the circulation of Qi and blood and improves the coordination of the activity of the brain with all the viscera.

The Significance of Relaxing the Body

As mentioned above, tension is harmful for the body. We need relaxation. Only when relaxation comes to the whole body can Qi flow freely through all the body's meridians, and blood circulate throughout the vessels; and only then can the nerves, muscles, viscera, and brain recover from tension, thus alleviating and eliminating dysfunctions of body and mind. It is confirmed by modern medicine that 50 to 80 percent of all bodily disease is stress-related, due to disturbances of the autonomic nervous system stemming from various stimulations in the internal and external

31

environment of the body. Modern medical theory regarding the higher activity of the cerebral cortex and nervous system holds that intense or harmful stimulation has an important influence on the physiology and pathology of the body and can cause diseases of the respiratory, circulatory, nervous, digestive, and endocrine systems. Some factors, e.g. tension, grief, fright and fear, can result in mental disorder, hypertension, gastrointestinal dysfunction, peptic ulcer, palpitation, shortness of breath, thoracic suffocation and pain, incontinence of urine and stool.

Nowadays, cancer is often seen as being related to mental and emotional factors. A person whose mind is depressed and melancholy is liable to have a body susceptible to cancer. Early in its history, Traditional Chinese Medicine isolated seven emotional factors— joy, anger, melancholy, mental activity, grief, fright, and fear— that have an important influence on the physiology and pathology of the body. These seven emotional factors are originally the normal physiological reactions to various stimulations of the internal and external environment. But when these stimulations are constant or excessive, they cause disease by influencing first the brain and, through it, the viscera. *The Yellow Emperor's Classic of Internal Medicine (Huang Di Nei Jing)* says:

> Excessive anger injures the liver; excessive joy injures the heart; excessive mental activity injures the spleen; excessive melancholy injures the lung; fright and fear injure the kidney.

Relaxation of the body can lower and eliminate or neutralize the harmful effects of excessive emotional stimulation and bring about a comfortable mental condition. Relaxing the body can be combined with regulating the breath and developing inner quiet to increase these positive effects. Relaxing the body and developing inner quiet first regulate cerebral activity and thus affect the viscera, thereby changing the pathological state of the body to a healthy one. It has been demonstrated in clinical physiological studies that working with inhalation in Qi Gong breathing practices can increase the excitability of the sympathetic nervous system (raising the blood pressure, quickening the heart rate, and slowing gastrointestinal peristalsis) while relatively decreasing the activity of the parasympathetic nervous system. Working with

Modern medical theory regarding the higher activity of the cerebral cortex and nervous system holds that intense or harmful stimulation can cause diseases of the respiratory, circulatory, nervous, digestive, and endocrine systems.

Relaxation of the body can lower, eliminate, or neutralize the harmful effects of excessive emotional stimulation and bring about a comfortable mental condition.

exhalation can promote the reactions of the parasympathetic nervous system (slowing the heart rate, reducing blood pressure, promoting gastrointestinal peristalsis) while relatively decreasing the excitability of the sympathetic nervous system. We therefore stress learning various methods of relaxational Qi Gong and paying much attention to exhalation during the early stages of practice. Exhalation combined with the intention to relax and remain inwardly silent strengthens the relaxing effect and plays an important role in regulating the autonomic nervous system.

Exhalation combined with the intention to relax and remain inwardly silent strengthens the relaxing effect.

Eliminating Bodily Tension

We will look at two kinds of bodily tension: tension due to emotion and tension arising from improper exercise.

Emotional tension: this may be caused by worry about one's disease symptoms or by unhappy or tense stimulations from the internal and external environment.

Tension due to improper exercise: tension may arise as a result of improper posture, over-seriousness of attitude, improper breathing, or being over-anxious to produce the effect of the exercise.

All these tensions can be eliminated by applying Qi Gong relaxation methods before performing exercises.

静

"Peaceful, Quiet"

2. Regulating The Heart/Mind (Xin)

Concerning Attention

Qi Gong exercises are mainly concerned with *attention* and Qi. Exercises that develop one's ability to control one's attention are said to be exercises of one's Heart/Mind and form a very important aspect of Qi Gong practice. By attention we mean both the experience of consciousness and the activity of the brain that lies behind it. Regulating attention allows the practitioner to bring his/her Qi into a comfortable condition. Finding this state of comfortableness and ease is the key to successfully applying Qi Gong to eliminate disease, strengthen the body, prolong life, and promote intelligence.

It is known in Traditional Chinese Medicine that cerebral functioning underlies two types of mental activity: *primordial* mind and *acquired* mind. Regulating the heart/mind controls the *acquired* habits of mental activity and attention that govern the "thinking" of the body. This regulation consists mostly of diminishing the activity of one's *acquired* mind in order to prevent the disturbance of *primordial* mind, and to maintain coordination and balance between acquired and primordial mind.

Primordial mind is congenital (inherited from the primordial vital energy and essence of the parents). Primordial mind dominates vital activity and is not controlled by sense, attention, or thinking activity. Acquired mind is formed through contact with the things of the natural world after birth. It dominates attention and thought. Primordial mind and acquired mind, however, are interdependent and interacting. If acquired mind engages in unlimited activity, it can become injured by the seven emotions and the six desires, resulting in damage to the brain and the internal organs, disturbance of Yin/Yang balance and Qi flow, disruption of blood circulation, and finally disease. One of the most important purposes of Qi Gong practice is to get rid of the disturbance of distracting thoughts by inducing a state of mental emptiness and calm through controlling attention and thought, thus inhibiting the acquired mind and preserving primoridal Qi.

Living in society, it is impossible for the body to be free from the seven emotions and the six desires. (The six desires are sex,

Heart/Mind (Xin)

35

money, fame, wealth, gain, and avoidance of loss.) It is also impossible to be free from worry and negative thought activity. Sun Simiao, a famous Tang Dynasty doctor and Qi Gong practitioner, said:

> If the body could be indifferent to clothes and food, sex and song, advantage and disadvantage, success or failure, wind and torture, gain and loss, but developed itself by exercising breath and Qi, it would experience long life. Although the body cannot be free from desires and thoughts, still desires and thoughts can be eliminated gradually.

It is impossible to live without some distractions. The problem is how to deal with them and control them so as to get rid of their disturbing quality.

Certainly, the body naturally has desires and thought activity. It is impossible to live without some distractions. The problem is how to deal with them and control them so as to get rid of their disturbing quality. Mental activity and thoughts are various. Some of them are benign, for instance, pleasant, relaxed, and happy thoughts. Some of them are malignant, for instance, angry, nervous, grievous, or unhappy thoughts. Benign thought activity and emotion may improve and regulate the processes of the excitement and inhibition of the cerebral cortex thereby helping to restore any impairment to the functioning of the five Zang and six Fu organs and helping to eliminate disease. On the other hand, malignant thought and emotion may disturb the functions of the cerebral cortex, resulting in a dysfunction of the internal organs and eventually causing organic disease. Qi Gong theory early recognized that benign thought activity has significant psychological and physiological affects. The ancient Chinese doctors accumulated a lot of experience and developed many methods in regard to this matter. In general, they found that the activity of thought must be easy and happy, carefree and content. Here are several of these ancient methods:

- When our mind is agitated, it is often useful to think of the beautiful scenery of nature—beautiful mountains and rivers, vast oceans, green land, the flourishing of spring, the silence of morning and moonlit night. We may imagine we are walking under the shade of a tree, or listening to lovely music; we may recall happy events in the past or think we are playing as children or listening

Zhu Gui, Clearing Up After Spring Rain, *(contemporary).*

to the song of birds and insects or the sound of mountain streams.

- We can use our imagination to correct unbalanced thoughts and feelings caused by changes in season and weather or to regulate directly our internal condition. In the unpleasant heat of summer, we may imagine heavy snow, cold weather, and the pine tree as it is in winter. During the passage of winter to spring, we may imagine the sight of ice and snow beginning to melt, and think that everything is coming back to life. In winter, we may think about a scene of flourishing early summer or the sight of beautiful spring. We may think of water and cold to eliminate heat in the body, and we may think of fire and heat to remove a chill.
- We may apply "relaxing action" to places in our body so as to get rid of distracting thoughts and induce inner quiet. By "relaxing action" I mean vibrating the limbs to cause them to relax, or moving the attention with an intention to relax from the head to the feet, thus removing distracting thoughts and regulating the breath.
- We may count our respirations and listen to the sound of our breathing, thinking "quiet" during inhalation and thinking "relax" during exhalation.
- We may concentrate on and observe various points on the body, such as Dantian, Mingmen, Yongquan, etc.

Keeping our attention on the abdominal Dantian can concentrate the mind, remove distracting thoughts, and induce inner quiet. Holding attention within the Dantian while practicing "abdominal breathing" may promote, collect, and transfer energy (primordial or Zheng Qi) in or into the place between the two kidneys (Mingmen) and then circulate it all over the body along the meridians. This is very important for strengthening the body and eliminating disease.

Wang Hui, After Chü-Jan's Brushwork, *1664 (see previous page).*

All the above practices serve to remove distracting or malignant thoughts. An often repeated Qi Gong principle is that we should have one thought instead of ten thousand thoughts: all thoughts can be turned into one. When we do this, our brain is brought into a state of inner quiet, we become indifferent to "fame or gain," and we experience a peaceful inner state of nothingness.

Holding Attention Within: The Function of Dantian

What does Dantian mean? Dantian is a term used both in Traditional Chinese Medicine and in Qi Gong. There are actually three Dantians, upper, middle and lower. When the term is used without qualification, it is the middle Dantian located in the abdominal area that is meant. The precise location of the middle Dantian varies from author to author. Sometimes it is said to be at the navel, sometimes 1.3 cun below the navel, and again, sometimes 1.3 cun interior from the navel (see page 69 for illustration of "cun"). We may think of the Dantian, however, not as a precise point but as a specific area, taking the navel as its center, the Zhongwan point (Ren 12) as its lower limit, and the Guanyuan point (Ren 4) as its upper limit. This area is what we will refer to as the Dantian.

Ancient Qi Gong practitioners considered the Dantian to be the place in the body where the "Dan" (the pill of immortality) could be obtained and refined.

According to Traditional Chinese Medical theories that unite the concepts of Yin/Yang, the five elements, Zang Fu organs, and meridians, the middle Dantian is associated with the spleen and the element earth. But the Dantian is connected to many other important bodily functions as well.

The Dantian connects with the Mingmen point and the two kidneys (Mingmen rules the kidneys). The kidneys store Jing (essence). The Original Qi energy of the San Jiao (Triple Warmer) is gathered from the place between the two kidneys (Mingmen) into the Dantian through special connecting meridians.

The Ren, Chong, Spleen, Kidney, and Liver channels pass either through the navel or around it, thus connecting with the Dantian area. The Ren Channel is the "sea" of all Yin channels; the Chong Channel is the "sea" of blood. Both Ren and Chong originate below the navel and interact with each other.

The Yin and Yang channels, associated with the interior and the exterior respectively, are connected to each other and are

> We may think of the Dantian not as a precise point but as a specific area, taking the navel as its center, the Zhongwan point (Ren 12) as its lower limit, and the Guanyuan point (Ren 4) as its upper limit.

interdependent. The Qi of the Zang Fu organs and their meridians can all be finally collected in the abdominal Dantian.

Ancient Qi Gong practitioners called the Dantian "the collecting place of the five Qi's," "the source of generating Qi" and "the root of life."

The Dantian has the following specific functions:
- regulates Qi
- reinforces primordial Qi
- strengthens the kidney (resulting in a strengthening of Jing and the body generally)
- regulates Qi in the vessels and the blood
- regulates Wei Qi (increasing one's ability to defend against disease)
- regulates the "Blood Room" (Chong channel, liver, and uterus)
- warms up the "Essence Palace" (place where Jing is collected in lower body)

Dantian acts as a pivot for transfering and storing Zheng Qi and for promoting the circulation of primordial Qi throughout the body along the channels and collaterals. To promote the functions of the Dantian, Qi Gong practice emphasizes holding one's attention in the Dantian and performing respiration exercises where long, deep breaths into the abdominal area to bring about a quieting in the Dantian. Holding one's attention in the Dantian has the following functions:

- helps bring about inner quiet
- helps develop abdominal respiration
- helps strengthen the spleen and stomach thereby promoting the functions of the other Zang Fu organs
- helps "empty out" the upper body and "fill up" the lower body

Dantain acts as a pivot for transfering and storing Zheng Qi and for promoting the circulation of Primordial Qi throughout the body along the channels and collaterals.

Developing Inner Quiet

The Meaning and Importance of Developing Inner Quiet

Developing Inner Quiet has a technical meaning in Qi Gong practice. It refers to the progressive diminution of distracting thoughts and the exercises that bring this about. In inner quiet the body is motionless and comfortable and dwells in a state of very light sleep; the mind is empty and the cerebral cortex is in a special state of protective inhibition.

As we have been discussing, the three main principles and methods of Qi Gong practice are "Regulating the Body" (training the posture), "Regulating the Heart/Mind" (training the attention), and "Regulating Respiration" (training the breath). All three serve the purpose of Developing Inner Quiet, which is itself a stage in "Regulating The Heart/Mind." Precisely how to concentrate the mind, making all the various thoughts become one thought and eliminating distractions, i.e., how to Develop Inner Quiet, is thus a very important question.

We should try our best to remove distracting thoughts and disturbances by freeing the mind from all negative thoughts during practice sessions.

We will now introduce several concrete methods for Developing Inner Quiet. The beginner in Qi Gong may find it difficult to keep the brain quiet and to eliminate distracting thoughts. This is the main barrier to success in Qi Gong. Therefore, we should try our best to take that barrier away. Learning to practice Qi Gong must have the definite purpose of: 1. strengthening the body and treating disease; 2. promoting intelligence and prolonging life. We should therefore try our best to remove distracting thoughts and disturbances by freeing the mind from all negative thoughts during practice sessions, i.e. personal troubles and difficulties at work, study, in the family, among friends, colleagues, and neighbors. This is an important step in inducing the brain to develop inner quiet.

The Concrete Methods for Developing Inner Quiet

Zhiguan Method: "Looking Within"

- Gazing along the nose or at the tip of the foot
- Letting the eyes gaze downward along the nose in the direction of the navel; at the same time gazing inwardly at the Dantian

Method of Keeping Attention Focused Within

- Keep attention focused either on the abdominal Dantian or on the Yonguan point or on some other specified point

Fu Ershi, Playing the Zither Along the Stream, (contemporary) (see next page).

42

臨流撫琴圖

丁卯十月傅聲遠於金陵師範待

Shifting and Guiding Qi Through Certain Activities of the Body

- Stirring the Sea (moving the tongue up, down, left, and right in the mouth)
- Sucking teeth (clenching the teeth, then sucking the molars, then sucking the incisors)
- Beating the Heavenly Drum (covering ears with two hands and snapping the two middle fingers against the occipital region)

Inducing Inner Quiet Through Regulating Respiration

- Counting breath: counting respiratory rate
- Hearing breath: listening to respiratory sound
- Paying attention to the breath, with the thought of quiet on the inhalation and the thought of relaxation on the exhalation
- Following the breath: keeping the attention on the breath as it flows in and out naturally

Imagination

- Imagining particular channels or points
- Imagining a certain thing or scene around the body such as beautiful scenery: ocean, blue sky, forest, or flowers. This is called the method of "holding attention on an outer scene."
- Recalling happy things from the past (including things that happened early in life)

Silent Reading Method

- Silently reading particular texts or poems

Inducing Inner Quiet by Listening to Sound

- Listening to gentle music
- Listening to the songs and sounds of animals and birds
- Listening to the tick tock of a clock or the sound of rain water flowing

Inducing Inner Quiet by Relaxing the Body

• Relaxing by vibrating
• Relaxing by tapping
• Relaxing by sense inducing

Method of Inducing Dantian/Abdominal Respiration

• Three partial inhalations with one complete exhalation
• Three partial exhalations with one complete inhalation
• Dantian inhalation method
• Inducing Inner Quiet through Massage
• Rhythmic massage applied to Dantian or other bodily area such as the four limbs, either by oneself or by doctor
• Massaging the nape of the neck and the coccyx-sacral area

We have introduced here many methods of inducing inner quiet. Each person should select a method according to his or her bodily condition. If during a practice session one has tried several methods and, due to emotional agitation or restlessness, one is still unable to induce inner quiet, it is a good idea to go for a short walk or practice some Qi Gong movements and then try again.

Illustrations from T'ai I Chin Hua Tsung Chih, "The Book of Conciousness and Life," *included in* The Secret of the Golden Flower *ed. by Richard Whilelm.*

Degrees of Inner Quiet

Inner Quiet in general can be measured from superficial to deep. There are three stages:

Inner Quiet, Initial Stage

This stage occurs when the mind is beginning to be concentrated. One has partially eliminated distracting thoughts, but not completely. At this stage, distracting thoughts may start up again after they have been temporarily pacified. The four limbs may experience a warm sensation and one's responsiveness to the external world begins to decrease.

Inner Quiet, Intermediate Stage

In this stage, distracting thoughts are obviously reduced or disappear completely, but one can still hear sounds from the external world. Warmth in the Dantian area and the four limbs gradually increases, and the body may feel that vital energy is

flowing. There will be some indication of the manifestation of Qi: warmth, distention, soreness, numbness, heaviness, coolness, itching, the sense of "insects crawling." There may be other physiological changes in the skin and muscle of some parts of the body.

Inner Quiet, Advanced Stage

In this stage, all distracting thought has stopped. The six sense gates (listening, inspecting, smelling, tasting, touching, and thinking) are now all closed. The eyes see nothing, the ears hear nothing, the brain has no thoughts. The whole body is in a condition where it experiences nothing but bare existence. This state gives one access to a very relaxing, easeful, wonderful, and silent realm.

The above three stages of Inner Quiet represent the process by which the Qi Gong trainee gradually progresses. The trainee must practice constantly in order to realize and master them.

3. Regulating Respiration

Respiration is foundation of vital activity. It is one of the central aspects of Qi Gong practice. Regulating respiration means regulating the breath until it is correct. The trainee of Qi Gong must master the breath. We will now discuss five topics concerning Regulating Respiration: 1. The significance of respiratory exercise; 2. Qi Gong for Regulating Respiration; 3. How to practice Abdominal Respiration; 4. More about the Pausal Breathing Method; 5. The question of reinforcing and reducing respiration in Qi Gong.

The Significance of Respiratory Exercise

Life cannot exist apart from respiration and the intake of oxygen from external nature. The body inhales oxygen and exhales carbon dioxide constantly in order to live. This process is called "getting rid of the stale and taking in the fresh." The cells of the cerebral cortex will cease to function if they are denied oxygen even for a few seconds. Therefore, health is profoundly affected by whether one breathes correctly and by how much fresh oxygen one takes in and how much carbon dioxide one lets out. That is why Traditional Chinese Medicine pays so much attention to respiratory exercise.

Respiratory exercises in Qi Gong are mainly concerned with abdominal respiration.

Respiratory exercises in Qi Gong are mainly concerned with abdominal respiration. Abdominal respiration promotes the flow of Qi and blood and prevents obstruction to that flow. It increases the volume of blood flow, improving the nutritional condition and general functioning of the whole body.

Slow, thread-like, smooth, deep, long abdominal respiration helps to calm the brain and induce inner quiet.

Slow, thread-like, smooth, deep, long abdominal respiration helps to calm the brain and to induce inner quiet. A quiet brain quiets the body, making it comfortable and happy, helping the body's tissues to rest and recuperate. Clinical experiments show that, in the state of inner quiet:

- The rate of brain wave activity in every region of the cerebral cortex diminishes, while the amplitude of alpha waves obviously increases and tends toward synchronization.

- Adrenaline decreases to 60 percent of normal; the secretion of other hormones, e.g. cortex hormone and growth hormone, diminishes.

47

- The rate of protein renewal slows down.
- Enzyme activation changes.
- Vascular tension is reduced.
- Oxygen consumption is 16 percent lower than in the waking state and 6 percent lower than in deep sleep.
- The lactate concentration in the blood is obviously reduced.

All these observations indicate that the metabolism of the whole body is reduced; the material basal metabolism of the brain and the body is slowed down; every cell and all tissues decrease in their consumption but increase in their storage of energy, a very significant factor in preservation of health and elimination of disease.

Qi Gong abdominal respiration regulates and exercises the functional activity of the viscera and the body generally. When the abdominal muscles and the diaphragm dilate and contract repeatedly, gastrointestinal peristalsis is promoted. This in turn promotes the activity of the heart, lung, liver, spleen, kidney, and urinary bladder, greatly increasing one's vital capacity, accelerating the process of inhaling oxygen and exhaling carbon dioxide, promoting the circulation of the blood, promoting the digestion and absorption of food, regulating the functions of the endocrine system and reinforcing resistance to disease. Obviously, the function of the lungs extends well beyond the exchange of gases. Two thousand years ago it was pointed out in the *The Yellow Emperor's Classic of Internal Medicine (Huang Di Nei Jing)* that

> the lung is the foundation of Qi and presides over the Zheng Qi of the whole body. Qi in the vessels flows into every channel and then returns to the lung.

This means that "the Qi of all the vessels originates in and returns to the lung through the opening and closing of the Shangzhong point (Ren 17)."

The lung has the function of dominating the Zheng Qi of the whole body. Modern medicine and physiology have confirmed this. The lung is a unique metabolic organ and has a function in the maintenance the intra-environmental stability of the body. It is closely related both to body metabolism and the secretion of certain hormones such as prostaglandin. It influences growth,

The lung is closely related both to body metabolism and the secretion of certain hormones. It influences growth, development, and reproduction as well as the body's ability to respond to change through the immune system.

development, and reproduction as well as the body's ability to respond to change through the immune system. The Shanzhong point, where lung Qi emerges and returns, is located exactly where the thoracic gland is found. The thoracic gland is related to the growth, development, and aging of the body. It itself is the earliest gland in the body to grow old. For these reasons, in Qi Gong practice, we emphasize keeping the attention in Dantian, abdominal respiration, "opening" and "closing" the Shangzhong point and holding one's attention there. Besides directly increasing vital capacity and promoting the circulation of the blood, pulmonary metabolism, and the secretion of hormones, opening, closing, and holding one's attention on Shangzhong has been reported to restore degenerative thoracic glandular functioning, bring smoothness to the movement of chest and diaphragm, regulate Qi, and calm the abnormal arousal of Qi. It can help with diseases of the heart and lung by clearing excessive moisture.

Slow, thread-like, smooth, deep, long, abdominal respiration plays an important role in regulating the autonomic nervous system of the body. It has been reported that 50 to 80 percent of all disease is stress-related, as we mentioned above. This implies that stress-related diseases involve disturbances of the autonomic nervous system. The interior organs of the body are controlled cooperatively by the sympathetic and parasympathetic nervous systems. Exhalation during Qi Gong practice can promote the work of the parasympathetic nervous system, while inhalation may promote the work of the sympathetic. Thus the practice of slow, thread-like, smooth, deep, long, abdominal respiration may help bring the autonomic nervous system to a state of dynamic equilibrium and health. As is well known, just as emotion has its effect on respiration, so respiration may be used to regulate emotion.

Qi Gong respiratory exercises, especially abdominal respiration, will promote the important activity of energy collection and energy storage that takes place in the area that has the abdominal Dantian as its center and includes the two kidneys and the Mingmen point. On the one hand, abdominal respiration promotes the production, action, and storage of primordial Qi and Zheng Qi, circulating them throughout the body along the meridians. On the other hand, it greatly decreases the basal me-

Abdominal respiration promotes the production, action, and storage of primordial Qi and Zheng Qi. It greatly decreases the basal metabolism of the body, thus reducing oxygen consumption.

tabolism of the body, thus reducing oxygen consumption.

Qi Gong for Regulating Respiration

The ancients called one single inhalation together with one exhalation one breath. For most people, respiration means thoracic breathing. Through the practice of Qi Gong respiratory exercises, the trainee experiences the sensation of respiration as extending deep into the abdomen. This is what is meant by abdominal respiration or Dantian breathing. As training develops, respiration can be further extended to what is called "foetal" respiration, "heel" respiration, and whole body respiration. This is a gradual, progressive process. In general, as we suggested above, the breathing during Qi Gong respiratory exercises must be thread-like, silent, deep, and long. It must be brought into the lower abdomen (Dantian) slowly.

Ancient doctors and Qi Gong trainees divided respiration into four categories or forms: Feng, Chuan, Qi, and Xi.

- *Feng* means wind. It is a breath where there is an audible sound during respiration.
- *Chuan* means wheezing or asthmatic breath. When this occurs, it means that the exchange of gases is incomplete.
- *Qi* means breath that is without sound or stagnation but that is still not thread-like and is not truly quiet.
- *Xi* is breath without sound or stagnation.

In Qi Gong practice, the result of Feng breathing will be dispersal; the result of Chuan will be stagnation; the result of Qi will be tiredness; but the result of Xi will be calming down. The first three forms of respiration are not gentle and smooth. When the breathing is thread-like, continuous, in action similar in appearance to the silk-worm emitting silk, only then is it said to be correct breathing. Qi Gong respiratory exercises have as their goal to bring about this fourth kind of breathing. Through regulating the breath in this way, the body relaxes more and more deeply, develops Inner Quiet, and eventually promotes the transference of Zheng Qi throughout the body, circulating it through the channels and collaterals. This is why so much attention was paid in the past to respiratory exercises of this kind. The ancient practitioners thought the duration and proper mastery of the breath to be the key, since it is this that directly influences the cultivation and promotion of Zheng Qi in the body. An ancient song says:

> The heart rules over the movement of the Qi.
> The Qi brings long life.
> When long and thread-like, smooth and continuous
> Breath flows in its circle,
> Disease can be removed and life prolonged.

Qi Gong respiratory exercises are divided into two types: natural respiration and abdominal respiration.

Natural respiration is simply quiet, natural breathing but there is a difference between natural respiration in Qi Gong and natural respiration when it occurs spontaneously. The features of Qi Gong natural breathing are as follows:

- It is based on the body's gradually becoming more and more relaxed.
- It is practiced in a state of mind where distracting thoughts have been initially eliminated.
- It is practiced in a state of even-temperedness wherein the mind becomes quiet gradually but without applying exertion or forced attention.

In *abdominal respiration* one feels that the breath is reaching down into the abdomen where a movement of rising and falling can be sensed during respiration. Generally, abdominal respiration has natural respiration as its basis and occurs in three types: natural abdominal respiration, deep, long abdominal respiration, and pausal respiration.

Natural abdominal respiration: This is a kind of natural breathing where the breath seems to reach into the abdomen without any special exertion or attention.

Deep, long, abdominal respiration: Here one concentrates on one's respiration. Each breath has the effect of inducing Qi through the trainee's paying attention to the movement of the abdomen and applying a bit of exertion to deepen and lengthen the breath. The respiration should be slow, long, thread-like, and even.

The above forms of abdominal respiration can be practiced in

51

two different manners: "conformal" abdominal respiration and "counter" abdominal respiration. In conformal-abdominal respiration, the abdomen bulges during inspiration and sinks during expiration. In counter-abdominal respiration, the abdomen sinks during inspiration and bulges during expiration.

When the trainee takes a deep, long abdominal breath, which one is to be used? It depends upon the disease-state and which form he or she finds natural. Most people choose conformal-abdominal breathing though a few naturally prefer the counter-type. Generally, the choice should be made naturally. The quantity of air and the exertion involved are greater in counter-abdominal respiration than in conformal. Therefore, older or more feeble persons, especially patients with hypertension or heart disease, should not use counter-abdominal respiration unless with great care.

Pausal respiration: on the basis of deep, long, thread-like, and even abdominal respiration, the trainee may develop pausal respiration. This means stopping the respiratory activity for a short time. There are two patterns:

1. Inhale – pause – exhale, making a brief stop between the end of inhalation and the beginning of exhalation.
2. Inhale – exhale – pause, making a brief stop between the end of exhalation and the beginning inhalation.

One should sustain the pause as long as one can without feeling tension or any sense of suffocation. Both types of pausal respiration function to promote gastrointestinal activity. The difference between them is that the first variety has the function of promoting the collection of Qi in Dantian, while the second variety functions to regulate the Qi in Dantian. In the clinic, one should recommend these patterns according to the individual case.

Generally, after a deep, long abdominal breath, there may spontaneously appear a short pause between exhalation and inhalation or between inhalation and exhalation. This is a good phenomenon and is a sign that the exercise has been practiced to a certain depth.

B ⫯ A

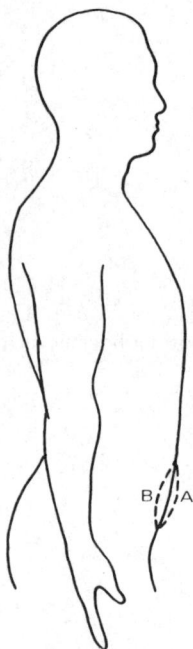

Counter and Conformal Respiration

How to Practice Abdominal Respiration

- Learning to practice abdominal respiration should take as its basis relaxed, quiet, natural breathing.
- On the basis of natural abdominal respiration, develop deep, long, abdominal respiration gradually until it is slow, quiet, thread-like and even.
- In the process of learning to practice abdominal respiration, the trainee must try to be relaxed, quiet, and natural, and neither to hold the breath or keep the attention fixed excessively. There should be no excessive exertion during practice.
- Learning to practice abdominal breathing must advance step by step. Be careful to avoid seeking to speed up to obtain effects. If the body is not first made accustomed to regulating respiration, abdominal respiration is impossible.
- For energy collection and storage in Dantian, the trainee may use additional methods such as "3 exhalations with 1 inhalation"; "3 inhalations with 1 exhalation"; and "7 times Dantian inhalation method." But these methods must be guided by a skillful Qi Gong doctor in order to avoid disorders due to improper respiration.

Practicing deep abdominal pausal breathing, one will come to feel that the breath is naturally stopping.

More About The Pausal Breathing Method

On the basis of the slow, quiet, thread-like, deep, and long abdominal respiration and the pausal respiration methods described above, a more advanced practice involves the interdependence of the heart/mind with the breath. While practicing deep abdominal pausal breathing, one holds one's attention on the breathing process. After a long time of practicing in this way, one will come to feel that the breath is naturally stopping. This is actually not a real stoppage, but a feeling, a sense that breathing has come to rest. At this point, inhalation is smooth and constant and exhalation is slight and long. The body only feels that energy is circulating throughout it, while the heart and brain feel very calm. This is called "gaining of breath in Zhi guan." The realm of Zhi is the realm of the interdependence of the heart/mind (Xin) and the breath. At this point one should look inward and keep looking inward. This is a realm for developing inner quiet as well as working with respiration. If one remains in this state for a long time, one may accumulate essence (Jing), Qi, and original Qi for the purpose of preserving health, strengthening the body, and treating disease. After gaining a certain amount of experience in training in this method, the trainee will gradually master it.

Reinforcing and Reducing Respiration in Qi Gong

In the case of a syndrome of the excessive type, one should take exhalation as primary. In the case of a syndrome of the deficient type, one should take inhalation as primary.

As is the case with herbal medicine and acupuncture, Qi Gong has methods for both reinforcing and reducing. Its achievement mainly depends on respiration: inhalation for reinforcing, exhalation for reducing. The principles are as follows.

- Greater inhalation with less exhalation is reinforcing while greater exhalation with less inhalation is reducing.
- Long inhalation with short exhalation is reinforcing; the reverse is reducing.
- Applying attention to inhalation is reinforcing; applying attention to exhalation is reducing.
- When exhalation is one third of inhalation, it is reinforcing; when inhalation is one third of exhalation, it is reducing.

When exhalation equals inhalation it is the even method. One applies respiratory reinforcing and reducing according to whether the syndrome being treated is due to an excess or a deficiency.

In the case of a syndrome of the excessive type, one should take exhalation as primary, i.e., much attention should be paid to exhalation. The duration of the exhalation should be long while that of the inhalation should be short.

In the case of a syndrome of the deficient type, one should take inhalation as primary, i.e., much attention should be paid to inhalation. The duration of the inhalation should be long and that of the exhalation should be short.

Generally, most patients with chronic disease have a deficiency syndrome with complications of the excessive type. In such cases, the respiratory method should be used flexibly according to the concrete state. Generally, at an early stage in practicing Qi Gong, the trainee should concentrate on exhalation in order to increase relaxation and quiet. After that, the trainee can work with inhalation. But overall, exhalation and inhalation should be equal and even. Don't be excessive.

III
QI GONG AND ASPECTS OF CHINESE MEDICINE

Symbols of Yin and Yang interacting through
the four seasons, Japanese, Early 19th Century

Modern Medicine and Traditional Medical Practices

Nowadays, medical practice is divided into two broad areas: Modern Medicine and the Traditional Medical Practices of various cultures. These two areas differ both in experimental method and intellectual approach. Although the history of its development is not long, Modern Medicine, using modern scientific techniques, has grown very rapidly and has made great contributions to the health and health care of humanity. Even so, Modern Medicine lacks radical methods for treating some chronic diseases and trails behind, in particular, Traditional Chinese Medicine (TCM) in methods for strengthening bodily resistance to disease, enhancing the functioning of the immune system, promoting intelligence, and prolonging life. In spite of the successes of Modern Medicine, Traditional Medicine still has much to offer.

Among the many medical traditions throughout the world, Traditional Chinese Medicine (TCM) has had the longest history and has been of the greatest influence. It has contributed much to health care, the prevention and treatment of disease, strengthening the quality of the body, and lengthening human life-span.

Qi Gong And Traditional Chinese Medicine

It is said that the history of the development of TCM goes back three thousand years. Actually, on the basis of literary documents discovered in recent decades, it can be inferred that Traditional Chinese Medical practices may go back as much as five thousand years. Throughout much of its history, TCM was called Han Medicine. Now it is known throughout the world as Oriental Medicine because, during the early Han and Tang Dynasties, it spread to all corners of Asia. The main components of TCM are Qi Gong, Chinese Massage, and Acupuncture-Moxibustion. Here we will be concerned primarily with Qi Gong. But the development and nature of Qi Gong is closely related to the other aspects of TCM. Many general concepts in TCM, such as the Five Elements, the Zang Fu organs, Qi, Spirit (Shen), Jing, Wei energy, Yin/Yang, theories of the circulation of blood and the transformation of Qi, are all related to the development and evolution of Qi Gong.

Daoist deity

57

In TCM, it is thought that vital activity is based on the fact that the human body responds to external nature. The universe is understood as a "big cycle" and the human body as a "small cycle." TCM stresses the coordinated action of the Qi of Yin and Yang, both in the universe and in the body. The universe is developed from both Yin and Yang. "All things in the universe are generated by the Qi of both Yin and Yang." In external nature, the sky is Yang and the earth is Yin; the sun is Yang and the moon is Yin; daytime is Yang and night is Yin; motion is Yang and quiescence is Yin. In the body, the body surface and its functioning belong to Yang while the interior of the body and the viscera belong to Yin; Qi, in general, is Yang, while blood, in general, is Yin, and so forth. Here, Yin and Yang represent two different attributes that pertain to all things and express a unity of complements.

In TCM, the Five Element Theory holds that everything in the world is composed of Five Essential Substances: metal, wood, water, fire, and earth. Metal is characterized by an upward tendency and represents a desire for free growth and strong activity. Wood is characterized by sprouting and branching, as is the case with trees and plants. Fire is characterized by Yang heat and a tendency to flare up. Water is characterized by cold-moisture and has a downward tendency. Earth is characterized as supporting, nourishing, and tending to change. The theory of Yin/Yang combined with the Five Element Theory is used to aid in observing human physiology and pathology and in guiding diagnosis and treatment. These theories also provide general principles for studying human life.

In regard to vital activity, it has been found that Zheng Qi (the anti-pathogenic factor), Yuan Qi (Primal Qi), and Interior Qi are the real dynamic factors in promoting the vital activity of the body. The occurrence and development of disease are directly related to the hyperactivity and hypoactivity of Zheng Qi. The earliest Chinese medical textbook, *The Yellow Emperor's Classic of Internal Medicine (Huang Di Nei Jing)*, pointed out:

> When a pathogenic factor has invaded, then the anti-pathogenic factor must be weak.

Traditional Chinese Medicine stresses the coordinated action of the Qi of Yin and Yang, both in the universe and in the body.

The Five Element Theory holds that everything in the world is composed of Five Essential Substances: metal, wood, water, fire, and earth.

Zheng Qi (the anti-pathogenic factor), Yuan Qi (Primal Qi), and Interior Qi are the real dynamic factors in promoting the vital activity of the body.

If the anti-pathogenic factor were reserved in the interior, the evil could not invade the body.

> It would be a syndrome of the excess type if there is a preponderance of the pathogenic factor, and a syndrome of the deficient type if there is exhaustion of essence and vital energy.

In order for the body to have an abundance of Zheng Qi and prevent the pathogenic factor from invading the body, it is important for the body to "avoid the pathogenic factor, keeping quiet and remaining indifferent to fame or gain, housing the mind in the interior. Then the Zheng Qi will stay with the body and the body will not succumb to disease."

These and other passages imply that we should pay attention to abnormal changes in the weather and practice Qi Gong carefully. Only in this way can the body remain in good health. But what exactly is this "Zheng Qi," the anti-pathogenic factor that the ancient text mentions? It consists of the Congential Jing (essence) and Qi (energy) inherited from one's parents, the Acquired Qi gathered through interaction with oxygen from the air, and the Jing Qi absorbed from food and nutrient material. All these together nourish the whole body. The *Nei Jing* says:

Daoist deity that rules the earth element

> What is Zheng Qi? It comes from one's parents and is associated with the Jing Qi of food. It is used to support and nourish the body.

Zheng Qi is stored in the two kidneys and generated in the Dantian. From the Dantian it is distributed to the five Zang and six Fu organs and to the whole body through the channels and collaterals. Vital activity depends upon the Zheng Qi's capacity for constantly promoting and nourishing it, and for restoring itself through getting rid of stale, and taking in fresh, Qi. In general, Zheng Qi carries out metabolism. Zheng Qi in the Zang Fu organs and in the meridians forms the Qi of the Zang Fu and the meridians.

The theory of the Zang Fu organs and the meridians deals with the most essential core of the body. It is the basis for guiding TCM in clinical practice. Qi Gong is primarily concerned with the exercise of the Zheng Qi of the body and the Jing, Qi, and Shen (spirit).

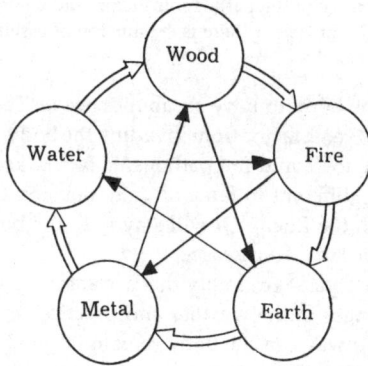

In TCM the five elements generate (empty arrows) and control (dark-pointed arrows) each other according to the above pattern. The elements also correspond with other aspects of existence according to the chart below.

	WOOD 木	FIRE 火	EARTH 土	METAL 金	WATER 水
Direction	East	South	Center	West	North
Season	Spring	Summer	Long Summer	Autumn	Winter
Climatic Condition	Wind	Summer Heat	Dampness	Dryness	Cold
Process	Birth	Growth	Transformation	Harvest	Storage
Color	Green	Red	Yellow	White	Black
Taste	Sour	Bitter	Sweet	Pungent	Salty
Smell	Goatish	Burning	Fragrant	Rank	Rotten
Yin Organ	Liver	Heart	Spleen	Lungs	Kidneys
Yang Organ	Gall Bladder	Small Intestine	Stomach	Large Intestine	Bladder
Opening	Eyes	Tongue	Mouth	Nose	Ears
Tissue	Sinews	Blood Vessels	Flesh	Skin/Hair	Bones
Emotion	Anger	Happiness	Pensiveness	Sadness	Fear
Human Sound	Shout	Laughter	Song	Weeping	Groan

Qi Gong and the Zang Fu Organs

"Zang Fu" is the general name for the viscera of the body. The viscera are divided into two groups of organs: five Zang organs including heart, liver, spleen, lung, and kidney; and six Fu organs including large intestine, small intestine, stomach, gall bladder, urinary bladder, and the tripple warmer. (Very roughly, the Zang organs have to do with the circulation and storage of energy and the Fu organs with digestion and elimination of waste.) Included in the Zang Fu classification are also the "extraordinary" organs, which are similar to the Zang formally and similar to the Fu functionally. The extraordinary organs include brain, marrow, bone, vessels, gall bladder, and uterus. The five sense organs (ears, eyes, mouth, nose, and tongue) and the five tissues (tendon, vessel, muscle, bone, and skin/hair) are also closely correlated with the Zang Fu organs. The five sense organs (together with the two lower orifices, comprising seven orifices in all) are the "openings" of the organs. The liver dominates the tendon and opens into the eye. The heart controls the blood and blood vessels and opens into the tongue. The spleen dominates the muscles and opens into the mouth. The lung dominates the skin and hair and opens into the nose. The kidney dominates the bones and opens into the ear. Through the channels and collaterals, the internal Zang Fu organs link with the body surface, the five tissues, and the sense organs, giving the body an organic integrity.

> "Zang Fu" is the general name for the viscera of the body.

The etiology and pathogenesis expounded by TCM pertain to diseases of Qi. There are two kinds of causes for disease: invasion by one of the six exogenous factors (wind, cold, summer heat, dampness, dryness, and heat-fire); interior damage due to the seven emotional factors (joy, anger, worry, melancholy, grief, fright, and fear).

> There are two kinds of causes for disease: invasion by the six exogenous factors, and interior damage due to the seven emotional factors.

In TCM, "all diseases are caused by Qi." In particular, disturbances of the seven emotional factors can affect the functioning of the Zang Fu organs, causing dysfunction of the interior Zang. In the *Nei Jing*, we find:

> A fit of anger may injure the liver; excessive joy may injure the heart; too much grief may injure the lung; too much

worry may injure the spleen; fright and fear may injure the kidney. Anger may result in an ascension of Qi; melancholy may cause an obstruction of Qi; grief may cause dispersion of Qi; worry may cause stagnancy of Qi; fright may cause descent of Qi; fear may cause disturbance of Qi; a disease of the Qi will lead to a disturbance of the blood; the disturbance of the Qi and the blood causes all other diseases.

Other causes of disease are irregular circulation of Qi and blood, obstruction of the channels and collaterals, and the struggle between pathogenic and anti-pathogenic factors. If the Zheng Qi (the anti-pathogenic factor) changes from strong to weak, disease will occur. Zheng Qi (mainly "indicating" Zheng Qi) circulates throughout the body along the channels and collaterals and is the foundation of vital activity. Qi Gong exercise, as we have said, is mainly intended to train, bring out, transfer, and strengthen the Zheng Qi of the body, thus strengthening Jing (essence), Qi, and Shen (spirit).

The names of the Zang Fu organs in TCM and Qi Gong correspond to the same organs in modern anatomy, but the physiological function of the Zang Fu organs and their pathological manifestations are different. The function of one Zang Fu organ in TCM may involve the function of several organs in modern medicine, while the physiological function of a single organ in modern medicine may involve several Zang Fu organs according to TCM. To see how this is, we will examine the give Zang organs.

The Heart: The main functions of the heart according to TCM are dominating the blood and blood vessels and housing the mind. The heart is a general pivot for the circulation of blood in the body. But it also controls the spirit and thinking. "The heart, where the mind is housed, is the king ruling over the five Zang and six Fu organs." A disorder of this "king" will endanger the other organs. This is the way the heart is understood in TCM.

Besides the function of the heart assigned to it by modern medicine, the heart of TCM also involves some of the physiological functions that modern medicine assigns to the nervous system. The brain function belongs to the heart in TCM because the theory of TCM takes Zang Fu as its core. Since the functions of

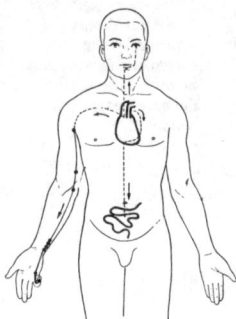

Heart Channel

62

the brain rely on nourishment by blood from the heart, the brain is included in the heart's functioning. In Qi Gong exercise, we put stress on regulating the heart, which implies nourishing the heart and mind, i.e, functions which are attributed to the brain in modern medicine. In fact, in Qi Gong, regulating the heart by means of the practice known as "Ru Jing," means making the brain quiet. Quieting the brain is one of the the three principles of Qi Gong exercise and is a key for both exercising the body and treating disease.

The Liver: The liver stores and generates blood. It has the function of regulating blood volume and maintaining patency for the flow of Qi. The digestion and absorption of food and emotional activity are both closely related to the liver. In Qi Gong exercise, we pay much attention to a series of training methods for harmonizing the liver, regulating its Qi and calming it, in order to promote vision (the liver opens into the eye) and tranquilize the mind.

The Spleen: The main functions of the spleen are governing transportation and transformation, absorbing essential food substances, and transmitting them to the whole body. The spleen also has the function of controlling the blood. In TCM and Qi Gong, attention is paid to the spleen in connection with the stomach. Whereas the kidney rules over one's innate constitution, the stomach and spleen determine one's acquired constitution. The terms, in TCM, refering to the stomach and spleen, include reference to modern medicine's gastrointestine, pancreas, and spleen. But they refer to other functions as well. The tissues and organs of the whole body rely on the stomach/spleen functions of transportation, transformation, and absorption to receive nutrients. Preponderance or discomfiture of Zheng Qi (including Qi of the Zang Fu and the meridians) are directly determined by the functioning of the spleen and stomach. In the clinic, after practicing Qi Gong for a certain amount of time, patients generally find their digestive functions, appetite, and general body quality improved. Improvement of the spleen and stomach promotes improvement of the other Zang Fu organs, e.g., heart, lung, liver, gall bladder, kidney, and urinary bladder, and these improvements in turn influence the whole body.

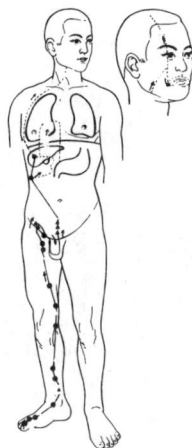

Liver Channel

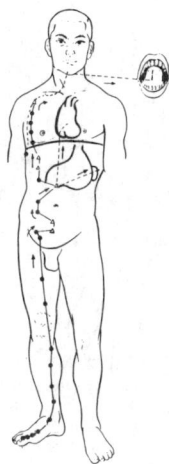

Spleen Channel

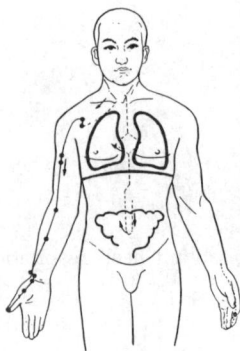

Lung Channel

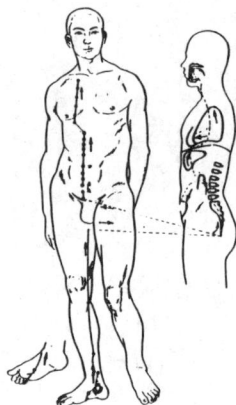

Kidney Channel

The Lung: The main functions of the lung are dominating the Qi and controlling respiration; dominating, dispersing, and descending as well as regulating water passage. Through respiration, the lung inhales clean Qi and exhales waste Qi. This is known as the function of "getting rid of the stale and taking in the fresh." This is indispensable to vital activity. The lung also controls the Zheng Qi of the whole body. It is not only the place where gases are exchanged, but it is also a special metabolic organ that is related to the body metabolism and the secretion of certain hormones that influence body growth, development, reproduction, and the immune system. In Qi Gong practice, we perform a respiration exercise, keeping our mind on Shanzhong (accupuncture point Ren 17, located on the midline of the sternum between the nipples), and then ascending, descending, opening, and closing that point. The purpose of this is to regulate and strengthen the lung function, thereby strengthening the Qi of the whole body.

The Kidney: The kidney dominates one's innate constitution. It is the foundation of the body's vital activity. It is located in the lumbar region. Between the second lumbar vertebra and between the two kidneys, there is a point (Du 4) called "Mingmen" which means "Gate of Life." Anterior to Mingmen is the abdominal point, Shenque (also known as middle Dantian), just below the navel. The energy stored in the place between the two kidneys is transmitted to the abdominal Dantian through the channels and collaterals. Between the two lower orifices, there is the Huiyin point (Ren 1, lower Dantian) at the perineum. 1.3 cun anterior to this point is a place for the male to store essence (Jing) and for the female to place Bao (the female Bao includes the uterus, ovary, and oviduct). The functions of the kidney are storing essence, dominating the bones, producing marrow, dominating reproduction, growth, and development, and regulating the water metabolism of the body. The two kidneys belong to the water element, but Mingmen (the gate of life) belongs to fire. Together they express kidney Yin and kidney Yang. The energy stored in the place between the two kidneys—the primal Qi of the San Jiao (tripple warmer)—originates from Mingmen and is the foundation of primordial energy. All the primordial energy (Yuan Qi) of the body is promoted by the energy stored in the place between the two kidneys. It can warm the Zang Fu organs and support the circulation and change of Qi of the San Jiao. It can warm the spleen and stomach and help digestion. It is closely related to the function of the sexual glands, in particular. In Qi Gong exercise, from ancient times until now, strengthening and exercising Mingmen and Huiyin, which are both closely related to the two

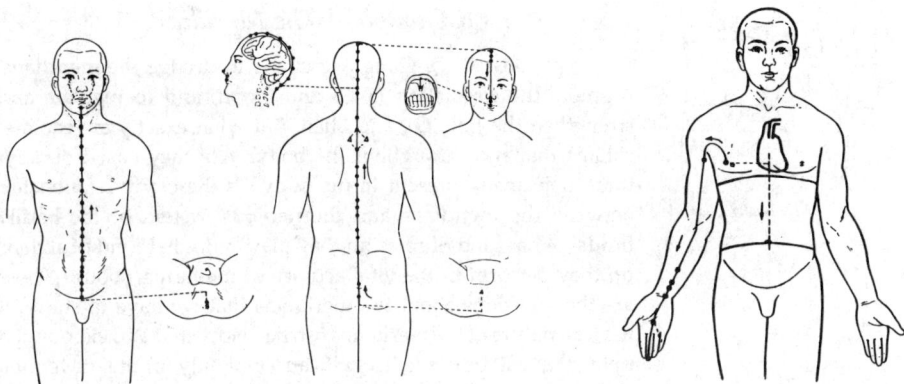

Ren Channel

Du Channel

Pericardium Channel

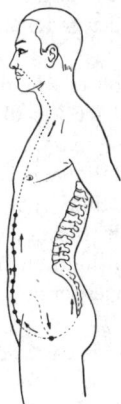

Chong Channel

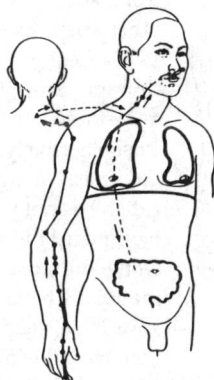

Large Intestine Channel

kidneys, are particularly stressed. In TCM and Qi Gong, the two kidneys, including the functions of Mingmen and Huiyin, actually summarize all the functions of the pituitary body and the adrenal and sexual glands, which are controlled by the hypothalamus in modern medicine. In other words, Qi Gong both exercises and reinforces the two kidneys, thus exercising and reinforcing the body essence (Jing), Qi, and Shen (spirit) as well.

Qi Gong and The Meridians

The purpose of Qi Gong exercise is to dredge the meridians, promote the circulation of Qi and blood, and to regulate and strengthen the Jing, Qi, and Shen. But what exactly are the meridians that run throughout the body? Are they based on anything objectively present in the body? Is there any relationship between the meridians and the nervous system or the bodily fluids? What kind of roles do they play and what kind of actions do they perform in the vital activity of the human body? These are the questions about the meridians that we have to study. If the true nature of the meridians can be discovered and expounded upon, this will be of great significance not only for the prevention and treatment of disease, the promotion of human intelligence, and the increase of human life-span, but it will also influence the future of Modern Medicine, biology, molecular biology, bio-control theory, physics, acoustics, optics, magnetics, electronics, and other scientific disciplines.

In recent years, biologists and other scientists have confirmed through data gathered in clinical studies of acupuncture, acuanaesthesia, Qi Gong, and Chinese massage, that the meridians exist objectively and that the Qi of the meridians have a substantial basis. Though the anatomical entity that constitutes the meridian has not yet been identified by histoanatomy and morphology, many phenomena regarding the transmission of sensation along the areas of the body corresponding to the traditional meridians have been verified.

In TCM, acupuncture and massage are used to increase the Qi, thereby inducing the transmission of sensation along the meridians and allowing the Qi to be guided to the diseased body area. Increasing the amount of Qi is the key. The more quickly the Qi

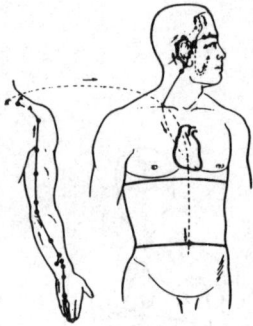

Triple Heater Channel

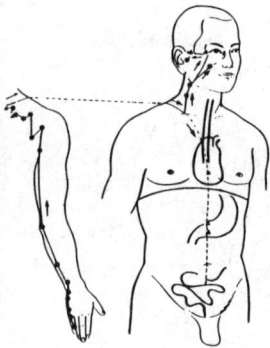

Small Intestine Channel

is produced and brought to the area, the better the effect. If no Qi arrives, there is no cure. In Qi Gong exercise, we pay a great deal of attention to the functioning of the Zheng Qi in relation to the Dantian. We emphasize increasing the quantity of Zheng Qi and moving it to the diseased area. This is one of the most important keys in Qi Gong for preventing and treating diseases, promoting intelligence, and prolonging life.

There is a close relation between the meridian system with its Qi circulating along it and both the nervous system and the regulation of the flow of bodily fluids. There is also a close relation between the meridian system and the bio-electro-magnetic field of the body. This is one of areas investigated in clinical and experimental studies. In recent years it has been demonstrated that Exterior Qi can be detected as a kind of electromagnetic wave produced by the human body. A number of studies have suggested that the meridian system is, indeed, related to the nerves, blood vessels, lymph, and endocrine systems. In some ways the functions of the meridians and these systems clearly over lap. Yet, though the meridian system is related to these phsyiological systems, it has its own unique character and plays a unique role in regulating vital activity. Some specialists argue that it, in fact, constitutes a regulatory system independent of the nervous, circulatory, lymph, and endocrine systems. For instance, it may play an important role in the formation of body tissue and organs and in regulating and controlling the functioning of these other systems. The true nature of the meridian system, from the point of view of modern medicine, is thus not yet entirely clear. We therefore have no choice but to understand and use it according to the theories of TCM.

According to TCM, the meridians are tubular in structure and distributed like ducts, rivers, and lakes throughout the body. They are connected to the Zang Fu organs interiorly and the four extremities and the body surface exteriorly, giving the body unity and integrity. They bear the responsibility for transporting and regulating Qi and blood throughout the whole body, nourishing the Zang Fu, tendons, bones, skin, and hair with Qi and blood, transmitting information and resisting pathogenic factors. "Meridian" is a general term for channels and collaterals. The system of the meridians, then, consists of twelve regular channels con-

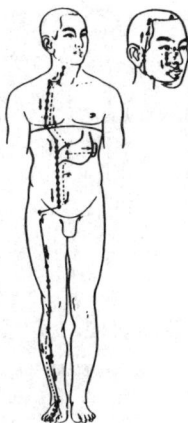

Stomach Channel

Gall Bladder Channel

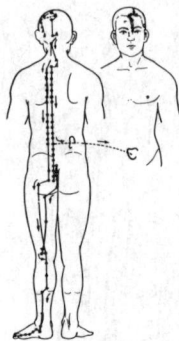

Urinary Bladder Channel

necting with the five Zang organs (plus the pericardium) and with the six Fu organs. It also includes eight extra channels, of which the Ren and the Du are the most important. The Ren channel goes along the midline of the front of the body and the Du channel goes along the midline of the back. The Ren channel is responsible for all the Yin channels, while the Du channel governs all the Yang channels. The Ren channel is called the "sea" of Yin channels; the Du channel is called be the "sea" of Yang channels. Both Ren and Du channels also govern and regulate all the Jing, Qi, and Shen of the body. These two channels, together with the twelve regular channles, are known as "the fourteen channels." The fourteen channels are the trunk and the core of the whole system.

During Qi Gong exercise, the mind (Yi) is often focused on important points along the fourteen channels, particularly along the Ren and Du. Another channel—the Chong (meaning "vital" and "pregnant," applied to this channel because it plays an important role during pregnancy) is also focused on in this way. The Chong channel overlaps and runs along with the Ren. It arises from the lower abdomen where the male stores semen and the female places the uterus. It is related to the genital system and has the function of regulating the Qi and blood of the twelve channels.

All the Zang Fu organs communicate with one another through the Ren, Du, and Chong channels. In Qi Gong exercise we pay a lot of attention to holding the mind (Yi) within and promoting the circulation of Qi through the Ren, Du, and Chong channels. The ancients thought that if the Ren and Du channels are unobstructed, all the channels will be unobstructed. Therfore, holding the mind within and promoting circulation through the Ren and Du channels are important for promoting and regulating the meridians, Qi, and blood of the body and for strengthening the body and treating disease.

In short, the meridian system is the pathway for the circulation of Zheng Qi in the body. It has the function of circulating Qi and blood, regulating Yin/Yang, nourishing the Zang Fu, tendons, bones, skin, and hair. It plays a very important role in all vital activity. It can be known through the practice of Qi Gong.

68

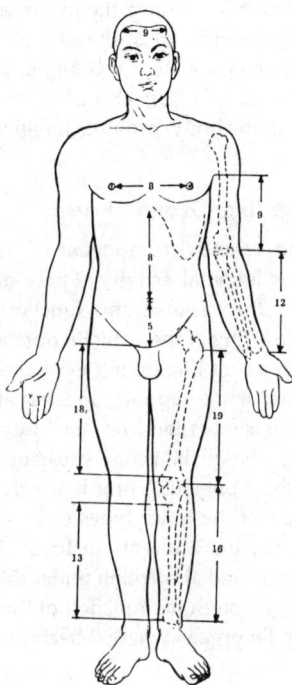

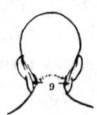

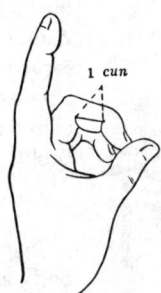

Measuring with
the middle finger.

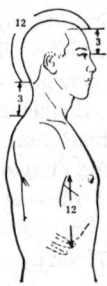

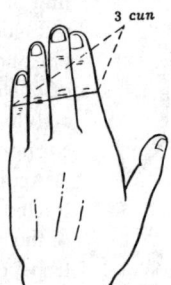

Measuring with
the four fingers.

*The measure used to locate acupuncture points is
determined relative to the proportions of the individual
body. The basic unit is the "cun." The diagram shows
different ways in which a length of 1 cun is measured.*

Qi Gong and The Three Treasures:
Jing, Qi, and Shen

精

Jing

气

Qi

神

Shen

Jing (essence), Qi (vital energy), and Shen (spirit) exist in every living thing. They are the substantial bases for vital activity and are the foundation for the formation and maintenance of life in the human body. Together with Yin/Yang, the five elements, the Zang Fu and meridians, they form part of the core of TCM and serve as a guide to clinical Qi Gong. But Qi Gong, in particular, stresses the direct exercise of Jing, Qi, and Shen in order to eliminate disease, strengthen the body, promote intelligence, and prolong life.

What are Jing, Qi and Shen?

Jing (essence): Jing is an essential component of the human body and serves as a basis for vital activity. Types of Jing are distinguished according to their source and function: there is congenital Jing, acquired Jing, Jing of the Zang Fu organs, and the Jing of reproduction. The types of Jing do not exist as four separate substances, but interact with, support, and transform into one another. Congenital Jing is inherited from the Jing and blood of one's parents and forms one of the prime substances of vital activity in the human body. Congenital Jing is involved in the support and transformation of the other types of Jing.

Acquired Jing comes from the nutrients in food. Jing is extracted from food by digestion and absorption under the auspices of the spleen and stomach. Through the function of the lung it is transported to all the Zang Fu organs where it becomes Zang Fu Jing.

Both Jing and Qi are stored in the two kidneys. The kidney also dominates the bone and produces marrow. The Kidney is the root of Qi. Qi Gong exercise stresses exercising Jing, nourishing Jing, and preserving Jing, particularly stressing exercise of the vital energy stored between the two kidneys. There are particular sets of Qi Gong exercises for concentrating the mind and exercising Qi, accumulating Qi to produce Jing, and strengthening the waist and Kidney.

In the practice of Qi Gong, attention is paid to increasing one's intake of nutrients in order to reinforce acquired Jing, and to keeping sexual activity at a moderate level in order to preserve congenital Jing.

Qi (vital energy): The meaning of the term "Qi" is very broad. Ancient Chinese philosophers, doctors, and scholars considered every vital activity in the world to be a function of Qi. Qi was considered to be the essential substance out of which the world is composed. The transformations of Yin and Yang Qi produce the various things existing in the world. "The body receives Qi and thus can live." "Life is due to the coming together of Qi and death is due to the dispersion of Qi." The body is within Qi and Qi is within the body. Thus all life depends on Qi. With Qi, beings live; without it, they die. It is a dynamic power promoting the activity of the human body. Qi coexists with Jing. Where there is Qi, there is Jing. Where there is Jing, there must be Qi. For this reason ancient scholars often refered to Jing and Qi together as "Jing Qi." In TCM, the circulation and transformation of Qi within the body is thought to operate according to its own law, undergoing processes of ascending, descending, going out, and transforming.

Qi is the essential substance out of which the world is composed.

Life is due to the coming together of Qi, and death is due to the dispersion of Qi.

Qi coexists with Jing.

The Qi in the body, the Zheng Qi, has three sources:

1. The Qi inherited from one's parents. This is known as Congential Qi.
2. The Qi derived from the air. This is mainly connected to the oxygen we breathe from the air.
3. The Qi acquired from food.

Both air-Qi and food-Qi are considered Acquired Qi. All three forms of Qi are indispensible for life.

Both Acquired Qi and Congenital Qi are stored in the kidneys. Through the respiratory action of the lung, the circulatory activity of the heart, the digestive and absorptive processes associated with the spleen and stomach, Acquired Qi and Congenital Qi are transported throughout the body.

Both acquired and congenital Qi are stored in the kidneys.

The Zheng Qi in circulation throughout the body has five significant functions:

1. Promoting function: Blood circulates through the body according to the "promotion" of the Qi. "Qi is the commander-in-chief of the blood, while blood is

71

the mother of Qi." Blood circulates along with Qi.

2. Warming function: Qi maintains normal body temperature, coordinating and balancing the body in relation to the environment.

3. Defending function: There is a passage in the *Nei Jing* that says:

> If a pathogenic factor has invaded the body, one's Qi must be deficient; if the Zheng Qi (anti-pathogenic factor) exists in the interior of the body, the pathogenic factor cannot make a successful attack. Thus, all disease, whether exogenous or endogenous, is related to the preponderance or discomfiture of Zheng Qi.

4. Astringent function: The sufficiency or deficiency of Jing Qi can control the dispersion of blood, sweat, and urine.

5. The function of the circulation and transformation of Qi: this function maintains the normal physiological activities of the Zang Fu organs and promotes the mutual interaction of Qi, blood, Jing, and body fluids.

As mentioned above, Jing and Qi are the substantial bases of the vital activity of the human body. They exist together. "The body will live when Jing Qi is present and die when it is exhausted."

In summary, Qi Gong exercise functions to strengthen the Zheng Qi by regulating the body, breath, and mind by keeping the mind focused within the Dantian through abdominal breathing; through ascending, descending, opening, and closing the Shanzhong (Ren 17), Dantian, and Yongquan (K.1) points; through circulating Zheng Qi in the Dantian, Mingmen, and Huiyin; and by concentrating the mind and training Qi and congenital Jing.

Shen: "Shen" means different things in different contexts. Most frequently it means spirit, mind, sense, or expression. Here it mainly means spirit or mind. Shen is also a general name for the vital activity of the body. It is the result of the highly concentrated activity of the brain and manifests outwardly as an expression of the Zang Fu, meridians, Qi, blood, Jing, and body fluids. It is derived from Jing and Qi, and like them it is has a substantial basis. It may be said that Shen is the outward manifestation of the cooperating action of Jing and Qi. Where Qi is strong, there will be Shen, where Qi is absent, Shen will weaken. Shen moves along with Qi and Jing is in its interior. The substance of Shen manifests in bodily appearance, while at the same time, Shen is a function of bodily appearance.

Shen depends on Qi and upon the existence of the appearance of the body to express its function. At the same time, the entire body—the brain, interior viscera, five sense organs and seven orifices, meridians, Qi-blood, Jing, and body fluids, even the movement of the body—all of these depend upon Shen to maintain their normal activity. The role of Shen is very broad. Because it plays such an important role in the vital activity of the body, it is said in the *Nei Jing*:

> Increase in Shen will result in life; loss of Shen will result in death.

Shen, thus, has the function of determining life and death.

In Qi Gong practice we pay a great deal of attention to preserving and training Shen. The exercise methods of nourishing the Heart/Mind (Xin) and calming, regulating, and preserving Shen are therefore developed. Three principle practices, i.e., regulating the body, regulating the breath, and regulating the Heart/Mind (Xin) have already been mentioned. In fact, the purpose for regulating the body and the breath is primarily to regulate the Xin. "Xin" here includes both brain and mind. By the three forms of regulation, the brain activity is inhibited and the body feels comfortable. This is the state known as "Inner Quiet." In the Qi Gong state of Inner Quiet, the brain cells are rested and their function is regulated because of the reduction of disturbance to the brain. The body metabolism generally is reduced and oxygen consumption decreases while the storage of energy increases. Through these means, the functioning of all the systems of the body are directly influenced and strenthened, and imbalance tends toward a relative dynamic equilibrium.

Among the functions of the Qi Gong state of Inner Quiet are the build-up, transfer, and strengthening of Zheng Qi. How can Qi Gong prevent and treat disease, promote intelligence, prolong life, and develop human potentialities? By regulating and nourishing the heart and the mind through bringing the brain to a

Congenital Shen dominates vital activity but is not controlled by mental activity, while Acquired Shen dominates mental activity.

quiet state and thus promoting a condition of active regulation.

Considered from the point of view of preserving health with Qi Gong, there are two kinds of Shen: Congenital Shen or Primordial Shen (Yuanshen) and Acquired Shen (Shishen). Congenital Shen is produced by the combination of male and female essence from the parents, uniting in the embryo. Acquired Shen refers mainly to mental activity. It is formed through contact with natural things after birth. These two kinds of Shen have different functions. Congenital Shen dominates vital activity but is not controlled by mental activity, while Acquired Shen dominates mental activity. They should work together and interact with each other to carry out normal vital activity. However, since human beings live in society and in a complicated environemnt and because we are disturbed by the seven emotional factors and six desires, we often are impelled to use our Acquired Shen frequently and without limit in ways that suppress and impair our Primordial Shen. Therefore, one of the important tasks of Qi Gong is to control the application of the Acquired Shen. This is accomplished by removing the disturbance of distracting thoughts and evil ideas and by inducing a state of Inner Quiet in which we can become indifferent to what in Chinese phraseology is referred to as "fame and gain." In this state we come to a sense of inner emptiness. This inner state has the capacity to suppress the activity of Acquired Shen to the advantage of Primordial Shen and further promote the intrinsic function of the latter. When the function of Primordial Shen is restored, there are definite benefits for health.

Because we are disturbed by emotions and desires, we use Acquired Shen frequently in ways that impair our Primordial Shen.

Inner Quiet suppresses the activity of Acquired Shen, and Primordial Shen is restored.

As we have been stressing throughout, Jing, Qi, and Shen play important roles in vital activity. Thus, the ancient practitioners of Chinese medicine and scholars specializing in methods of preserving health paid particular attention to the preservation and exercise of these three fundamental substances. Jing, Qi, and Shen do not exist in isolation. They coexist in the same body and cannot be separated. The Ancient doctors pointed out that Shen moves along with Qi and that Jing exists in the interior of the Shen. The longevity of the body depends upon the care and preservation of Jing, Qi, and Shen.

"Accumulate Shen to promote Qi and accumulate Qi to promote Jing; refine Jing until it becomes Qi; refine Qi into Shen;

74

refine Shen to emptiness." This is the way to strengthen, support, and increase the Jing, Qi, and Shen of the body.

How Does Qi Gong Exercise Jing, Qi, and Shen?

Qi Gong exercises for Jing, Qi, and Shen involve keeping one's senses focused within and exercising and regulating the meridians and the acupuncture points along them, in particular, the abdominal Dantian, Mingmen (Du 4), and Huiyin (Ren 1). These points, as we have seen, are all related to the two kidneys.

Holding one's attention within the abdominal Dantian strengthens the Shen and Qi. Holding one's attention on Mingmen and Huiyin refines Jing (including Blood-Jing and the Jing of reproduction) as well as refining Shen and Qi. The abdominal Dantian (with the umbilicus as its center), Mingmen, and Huiyin are closely related to the two kidneys and through them to the other Zang Fu organs and all the meridians of the body. Let us look at the functions of the Dantian, Mingmen, Huiyin, and Kidneys one by one.

Dantian: Here, we are refering to the abdominal Dantian. "Tian" means field. It is a place of sowing and reaping. The Dantian is not a point, but a general area. Its upper bound is Zhongwan (Ren 12) and its lower bound is Zhongji (Ren 3). This area is generally known as Dantian. Through it pass the Ren, Chong, Kidney, Stomach, Liver, and Spleen meridians. Because of the way the interior and the exterior of the body relate to each other and because of the interdependence of Yin and Yang energies, as well as the way the meridians are connected to the Zang Fu organs, the Zheng Qi of the Organs and meridians of the whole body can collect in the abdominal Dantian.

Ancient doctors called this Dantian "the place where the five Qi's return to their origin" and "the place where the Zheng Qi of the five Zang organs collect together." They also called Dantian "the source of generating Qi" and "the root of life."

The important functions of the Dantian are regulating and reinforcing Qi, strengthening the spleen and stomach, reinforcing the kidney, preserving Jing, regulating Yin-Wei (the two kinds of Qi), regulating the "Blood Room" (the Chong channel, liver, and uterus), and warming the "Essence Palace" (the place where Jing collects). The energy stored in the place between the two kidneys

Holding one's attention within the abdominal Dantian strengthens the Shen and Qi.

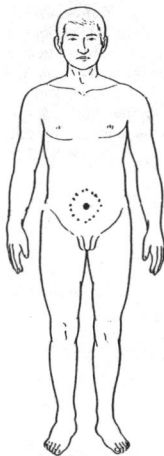

Dantian is not a point but a general area. Its upper bound is Zhongwan (Ren 12) and its lower bound is Zhongji (Ren 3). Through the Dantian pass the Ren, Chong, Kidney, Stomach, Liver, and Spleen meridians.

75

(the Primordial Qi of the Triple Warmer) is also collected in the abdominal Dantian through special connections among the meridians. Dantian therefore becomes an important central location where the generation, collection, storage, and circulation of the Zheng Qi of the whole body can be promoted.

Mingmen: "Mingmen" means "Gate of Life." It is an important point on the lower back along the Du channel. It is located below the second lumbar vertebra between the two kidneys and posterior to the umbilicus. It is called "the posterior Dantian" by some scholars. Mingmen "leads" the kidneys. Existing precisely between them, it affords communication between the kidneys, the umbilicus, and the heart, lung, and brain above. It is a source of vitality and the ruler of the "Xiang fire"—the fire from The Gate of Life—and of the Essence Palace. Mingmen is a "sea" of Jing and blood, as compared to the spleen and stomach, which are "seas" of water and food, respectively. Both serve as the foundation of the five Zang organs, for only through them can the Yin-Qi and Yang-Qi of the five Zang organs be generated and developed. At the same time, while Mingmen belongs to fire, the two kidneys, with which it is closely associated, belongs to the element water. In the pair, fire/water, fire rules water while water is the origin of fire. Water and fire must support each other. They are interdependent and cannot be separated. Kidney's Water and and Mingmen's Fire are known as Primordial Yin and Primordial Yang. Together they comprise Congenital Jing Qi. When Primordial Yin and Yang are regulated and brought to balance, they can further regulate and equilibrate the Yin and Yang of the whole body.

Huiyin (Ren 1): This point is found on the perineum. It is the point of origin of the Ren, Du and Chong channels, located precisely between the anus and the urethra. It was called "The Sea Bottom" and "The Lower Dantian" by ancient doctors. It is said to be the source of Reproduction-Jing. It is thus related to the genital functions of both sexes. In an ancient text we find: "The place 1.3 cun anterior to the Huiyin point stores Jing (in the sense of semen) in the male and is the place of the uterus in the female." Doctors and Qi Gong practitioners in years past considered the two kidneys, Mingmen, abdominal Dantian, and Huiyin as an

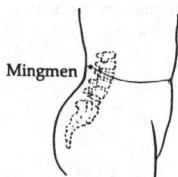

Mingmen

"Mingmen" means "Gate of life." It is known as the posterior Dantian. It is connected to the kidneys. While Mingmen belongs to fire, the kidneys belong to water. Through the association of Mingmen and kidneys, water and fire support each other.

Huiyin

inseparable whole that functions as a regulative center for all vital activity. It has been demonstrated by an abundance of clinical data that stimulating the adbominal Dantian together with Mingmen and Huiyin can directly affect the secretory activity of the pituitary, adrenal, and sexual glands, thus activating, in terms of TCM, Kidney Yin and Kidney Yang. Modern medical studies associate deficiency of Kidney Yin or Yang or both Yin and Yang with a dysfunction of the hypothalamus—the gland that controls the endocrine system and regulates, for instance, the flow of pituitary, adrenal, and sexual secretions. Such dysfunction or deficiency manifests as a decline in physiological function caused by a deficiency of hormonal secretion.

Kidneys: Doctors and Qi Gong scholars of the past have stressed that the kidney is the foundation of life. "The Kidneys, by storing essence and dominating bone, by producing marrow and promoting intelligence, are the root of Qi." All the Jing Qi of the five Zang and six Fu organs are stored in the two kidneys and converge in the abdominal Dantian. The two kidneys are important parts of the regulating center of vital activity and are closely related to the growth, development, reproduction, and aging of the human body. As a matter of fact, these functions of the Kidney as understood by TCM are an amalgamation of some of the functions of the brain and endocrine system of modern medicine—including, of course, the functions of the pituitary, adrenal, and sex glands.

It has been confirmed by many clinical studies that Qi Gong exercise begins by affecting the function of the autonomic nervous system and goes on to balance the sympathetic and parasympathetic systems. From there, Qi Gong goes on to influence every system of the body from the central nervous system to the functional activities of the respiratary, circulatary, digestive, urinary, and genital systems. While Qi Gong exercise is mainly concerned with holding one's senses within the body and exercising the abdominal Dantian, Mingmen, and Huiyin (which, as stated above, together with the two Kidneys, serve as the center for regulating vital activity), these practices in modern medical terms serve to regulate the function of the cerebral cortex. One

The kidneys, by storing essence and dominating bone, by producing marrow and promoting intelligence, are the root of Qi.

can also think of Qi Gong practice from the cybernetic point of view: preserving and training Jing, Qi, and Shen generalizes the self-regulating functions of the body and brings cybernetics down from theory to practice. Through the regulation of body, breath, and heart/mind, the various forms of information coming from the inner and external environments —information that stimulates and disturbs the brain—can be responded to effectively, thus protecting and strengthening the self-stabilizing, dynamic equilibrium of the body's control system.

Anonymous, A Bridge Over a Stream Among Steep Mountains,
Early 13th Century

Modern Medical Studies on Qi Gong

Studies Regarding "Regulating the Body"

Why do we practice regulating the body, i.e., why should we regulate our posture and perform special movements in Qi Gong? Because achieving correct posture at the outset is the best way to develop relaxation and get into a state of Inner Quiet. Relaxation and Inner Quiet are the central Qi Gong practices. Mastering them is the most important factor in influencing and changing the physiology and pathology of the body. From the point of view of modern medical science, regulating posture has certain definite physiological effects:

- Certain postures and movements may regulate the strength of the skeletal muscles of the whole body and directly influence dynamic changes in the circulation and reassignment of the blood.
- Certain postures and movements excite the motor centers and inhibit the cerebral cortex of the brain.
- Certain postures and movements influence the function of the autonomic nervous system, removing smooth-muscular spasms of the esophagus and large intestine.

Let us look at the posture known as "Standing Stake Exercise" as an example. Different variations on the Standing Stake Exercise may cause different influences on the body. In the "V" version of the form, the point of gravity is the sole of the foot at the Youngquan point, (K 1). This posture is excellent for exercising the Ren channel. In the "A" version of the form, the point of gravity is on the heel. This is beneficial for the Du channel.

It has been confirmed through the scientific study of the various categories of bodily posture (walking, standing, sitting, lying down, and kneeling) that training and exercising different parts of the body in different ways causes different effects on the body. The details of these effects will be dealt with later in this chapter.

Studies Regarding "Regulating Breath"

The purpose of regulating respiration is to make our breathing correct. Accomplishing this is one of the three principles of Qi

Gong. Regulating respiration not only affects the results of Qi Gong practice but is also a very important way of building up and exercising the Zheng Qi of the body and inducing quiet in the brain. Generally, breathing in Qi Gong involves keeping the breath smooth, quiet, fine, deep, and continuous. It is usually abdominal breathing. Only after the slow, quiet, slender, deep, and long abdominal breath is mastered can the observable physiological changes be produced in the body. When training in regulating the breath has been accomplished, the physiological changes that result are numerous.

First of all, Qi Gong breathing promotes the functioning of the respiratory muscles. The active range of the diaphragm muscle obviously increases to two to four times that of the normal body. This greatly increases pulmonary vital capacity and improves the blood circulation of the heart and lung. The amount of carbondioxide exhaled from the pulmonary alveolus is increased while the exhalation of oxygen is decreased. This is a special feature of Qi Gong breathing which, through increasing the amount of available oxygen, helps put the body into a relaxed and quiet condition. One's breath is unhindered and one feels comfortable all over the body. Because the oxygen content in the pulmonary venous blood increases while carbondioxide diminishes, blood circulation is improved. The volume of blood flow increases while the per-minute respiratory frequency is greatly reduced, resulting in a reduction of the heat energy required for gaseous exchange to take place. This leads to an increase in the amount of energy stored in the body. Oxygen is increased, energy consumption diminished. The respiratory rate for a normal body is sixteen to eighteen breaths per minute. The Qi Gong practitioner may find that his or her breathing rate decreases to eight, six, four, two or even one breath per minute during practice. This demonstrates that Qi Gong can obviously change and regulate the functioning of the regulatory center.

As one practices regulating respiration, the movements of the abdominal muscles and diaphragm will increase. A skillful Qi Gong practitioner may increase the active range of the diaphragm to 12 cm, three or four times that of the normal, untrained body. The movements of the diaphragm and the abdominal muscles

80

will directly influence the blood volume of the liver and blood circulation generally, as well as the physiological functioning of the liver and gall bladder. The movements of the abdominal and diaphragm muscles massage the internal organs—especially the stomach, pancreas, and intestines. This further tends to improve blood circulation throughout the digestive system and enhance the secretion and absorption of gastroentestinal and pancreatic fluids. The effects of Qi Gong are therefore perfect for disorders of the digestive system revealed in the clinic. Abdominal breathing combined with holding one's attention within the abdominal Dantian can further strengthen and improve the functioning and blood circulation of the pelvic organs and lumbosacral tissues.

Regulating the breath with slow, quiet, slender, deep, and long abdominal breathing is also a method for adjusting the autonomic nervous system and through this for regulating the activity of every organ. Clinical and physiological experiments have demonstrated that inhalation in Qi Gong breathing promotes the excitation of the sympathetic while exhalation increases excitement of the parasympathetic nervous systems. Based on these findings, it is clear that people can regulate and balance the sympathetic and parasympathetic nervous systems through strengthening their inspiration and expiration. It has also been demonstrated that from fifty to eighty percent of all incidences of diseases such as hypertension, some forms of heart disease, peptic ulcer, and neurasthenia have their causes in the dysfunction of the autonomic nervous system. We can infer, therefore, that Qi Gong is the perfect therapy for regulating such disorders.

Recently, Chinese scholars have hypothesized that the excitement of the sympathetic nervous system is analogous to the hyperactivity of Yang (or the deficiency of Yin) as described by TCM, while excitation of the parasympathetic nervous system is analogous to deficiency of Yang (or hyperactivity of Yin). Since Qi Gong has the function of regulating and equilibrating the Yin and Yang, we can understand how it can be effective in balancing the nervous system.

Studies Regarding "Regulating Heart/Mind (Xin)"

In the phrase "regulating the Heart/Mind (Xin)," "Xin" refers to the brain in its capacity as ruler of all the organs where the

In Qi Gong, the brain becomes regular in its functioning so that the cerebral cortex can enter a relaxed state.

mind is housed. In Qi Gong, making the brain become regular in its functioning so that the cerebral cortex can enter a relaxed state— the state of Inner Quiet—is an important key for removing diseases, maintaining health, promoting intelligence, prolonging life, and actualizing the potentialities latent within the body.

Clinical experiments have demonstrated that the cerebral cortex can pass from a tense and excited state to a relaxed and calm state through regulating the brain and entering into Inner Quiet. When the cerebral cells are relaxed and calm, the blood volume of the brain is increased and its blood circulation is improved so that the oxygen content of the brain rises. This is extremely significant since the brain requires more blood and oxygen than any other tissue in the body. If ischemia and anoxia occur even for a few seconds, there will be severe results. As the blood circulation in the brain is improved, the blood volume and volume of oxygen are increased and the brain cells gain a sufficient amount of nutrition. This strengthens the functioning of the cerebral cortex and promotes the development of latent potentialities as well as improves indirectly the functioning of the whole body.

Observations of changes in brain waves conducted through electroencephalogram (EEG) show that after entering a state of Inner Quiet, the alpha wave activity increases. The brain-wave frequency in every region of cortical cells slows down and its rhythm becomes more steady and synchronized in a more orderly fashion. For normal persons, the brain waves of the many regions of the cerebral cortex are not synchronous and the wave amplitude is not more than 50 microvolts. But after practicing Qi Gong, the wave range can increase to 150 to 180 microvolts. Also, slow theta waves appear and spread, and the even slower delta waves manifest. These experimental observations demonstrate that after achieving Inner Quiet, cerebral cells are in a state of protective inhibition. This benign inhibition spreads to every cell of the cortex. This provides rest for the brain's nerve cells and has a regulating and repairing function for the brain and the whole body.

Experimental observations demonstrate that after achieving Inner Quiet, cerebral cells are in a state of protective inhibition.

When one has regulated one's heart and entered a state of Inner Quiet, biochemical bodily change manifests as a clear reduction of cerebral basal metabolism, which, in turn, influences

When the cerebral cortext is in a state of Inner Quiet, the secretion of adrenaline is 60 percent lower than normal.

the basal metabolism of the whole body. Experiments have demonstrated that when the cerebral cortex is in a state of Inner Quiet, the secretion of adrenaline is 60 percent lower than normal. Secretions of other hormones, such as cortex steroid and growth hormone, clearly increase. The renewal rate of protein slows down, vascular tension reduces, and cholesterol decreases. In Inner Quiet, oxygen consumption by the brain per unit of time decreases to a rate 16 percent lower than that of a normal waking body and 6 percent lower than a normal body in sound sleep. Metabolism of the central nervous mediator (5-HT) is two to three times higher than normal, (5-HT has the function of inhibiting the cerebral cortex and at the same time has a self-regulating feedback function) but hydroxytramine and skin potential are reduced. This means that the metabolism of the brain and of the tissues of the whole body slows down. Consumption decreases but energy storage increases. Because harmful stimulation from the intra-exo-en-vironment disturbing the brain is eliminated or reduced, the central nervous system is repaired, regulated, and balanced. This is very important in preventing and treating disease, promoting intelligence and long life, as well as developing the latent potentialities of the body.

The metabolism of the brain and of the tissues of the body slows down. Consumption decreases but energy storage increases.

It has been demonstrated by clinical study that after regulating the Xin and attaining a state of Inner Quiet, the brain function clearly improves. Powers of memory, arithmetical calculation, observation, and discrimination are increased.

Powers of memory, arithmetical calculation, observation, and discrimination are increased.

Regulating the breath and heart in Qi Gong may influence the heart rate, blood circulation, blood pressure, skin temperature, and blood compounds. The heart rate slows down during Qi Gong (generally, about 10 times per minute slower than normal). This indicates a reduction of the excitability of the sympathetic nervous system that controls the heart. The patient with hypertension practicing Qi Gong can reduce blood pressure. The relaxation and quieting down of the body affects the autonomic nervous center, which causes the vascular motor center to become steady. The skin temperature usually rises very obviously in the region of the Dantian and the points on the hands. Generally, skin temperature may rise two or three degrees centigrade, as determined by "blood flow pictures." The volume of blood flow in the upper limbs may increase 30 percent, as shown by "thermal imaging pictures" while the infrared radiation of the palm also markedly increases. The thermal picture turns from dark to bright red. The elevation in skin temperature shows where the skin vessels are dilated. This is a manifestation of a reduction in sympathetic nervous tension. Changes in blood compounds after training are also found. Erythrocytes (red cells), thrombocytes (clotting cells), and eosinophilic granulocytes (white cells) increase, indicating that Qi Gong can affect the hematopoietic function (blood production). Further, the phagocytosis of leukocytes and some bacterial opsonin and the phagocytic index increase. This indicates that Qi Gong promotes the defensive functioning of the immune system.

Qi Gong promotes the defensive functioning of the immune system.

In recent years, researchers have studied the serums CAMP and bile secretion during Qi Gong. It has been found that Qi Gong may influence the CAMP content and bring it to steadiness. The increase in CAMP content makes the mediator that transmits information increase. Bile secretion during Qi Gong practice may be two or three times that of normal.

Studies Regarding The Substantial Basis of Exterior Qi in Qi Gong

Early in the spring of 1978, Qi Gong doctor Lin Hou-Sheng of Shanghai Qi Gong Research Institute and Gu Han-Sheng of Shanghai Atomic Nuclear Research Institute cooperated to study the substantial basis of Qi in Qi Gong practice. Definite physical and physiological effects were discovered. It was found that exterior Qi is characterized by strong infrared energy, the flow of microparticles, the appearance of visible light, static electricity as well as ultraviolet and microwaves.

In a study reported by The Automatic Research Institute of the Chinese Academy of Science, computor analysis demonstrated that exterior Qi involves coding and informational structures.

Experimental study by Shanghai Communications University showed that during Qi Gong practice the body releases a certain energy or substance that was dubbed "the body field." These energies and substances can function as information transmissible through space and can be received by another person.

Exterior Qi has a substantial basis.

Thus, the exterior Qi of Qi Gong does seem to have a substantial basis. Recently, in China, the Exterior Qi of Qi Gong, besides

84

being studied scientifically, is being used in the clinic. It definitely has an affect on some tumors, brain trauma, gastroentestinal disorders, disorders of the neck, chest, and lumbar vertebrae and some ocular problems, e.g., young myopia. Exterior Qi is particularly effective in the relief of pain. In surgical operations on thyroid tumors, anaesthetization by exterior Qi has the same effect as acupuncture. Exterior Qi (considered as an infrared, electromagnetic, information-carrying wave) has become an important clinical instrument. Of course, this instrument—the exercising, distributing, transporting, and reinforcing Qi—has been used in TCM for thousands of years and deserves further scientific study.

Exterior Qi has become an important clinical instrument.

In summary, the practice of Qi Gong is guided by three principles: regulating the body, regulating the respiration, and regulating the heart/mind. Regulating the body, respiration, and heart/mind are very important during Qi Gong practice and can directly affect the functioning of the central and autonomic nervous systems. While in a state of Inner Quiet, the body experiences physical changes that manifest mainly as a reduction of basal metabolism, oxygen consumption, and blood pressure, a slowing down of respiratory frequency, as well as a quickening of gastroentestinal peristalsis. These effects indicate that Qi Gong functions well to improve disorders of the body and the heart/mind.

Liu-hai, the Immortal, 18th Century

Daoist Immortal Liu-hai by Yen Hui, 14th Century

In the various clinical and experimental studies mentioned above, Qi Gong has been shown to have the function of regulating and strengthening the self-controlling capacity of the body. It is highly effective in rehabilitation and promoting rest. Qi Gong allows the body to increase its absorption of nutrients without gain in consumption. Therefore, Qi Gong acts to preserve energy. It gives the body every advantage. This is the main point of Qi Gong: that it can eliminate disease, strengthen the body, promote intelligence, prolong life, and develop the latent energy of the body.

Daoist Immortal

List of Names and Titles

PENYIN	CHINESE	ENGLISH
Bao Puzi	抱朴子	*Bao Puzi's Inner Treasure*
Bai Ju-yi	白居易	Bai Ju-yi (Po Chu-i)
Bai Zi Bei	百字碑	*One Hundred Word Tombstone*
Bianque	扁鵲	Bianque
Bi Gu Shi Qi Fa	辟谷食氣法	*Method of Eliminating Food-intake and Promoting Qi Circulation*
Bing Hou Zuo	病後作	*Works After Sickness*
Can Tong Qi	參同契	*Commentary on The Book of Changes*
Cao Yuanfang	曹元方	Cao Yuanfang
Chang Sheng Shi Liu Zi Jue	長生拾陸字訣	*Sixteen Words for Acquiring Longevity*
Changsha	長沙	Changsha
Chen Xu Bai	陳虛白	Chen Xu Bai
Chen Zhi	陳摯	Chen Zhi
Chu Ci Yuan You	楚辭·遠遊	*Wandering Far Away*
Dao	道	The Tao, The Way, Taoist School
Dao De Jing	道德經	*The Way and Its Power*
Dao Yin Ge Jue	导引歌訣	*Guarding Sounds*
Dao Yin Tu	导引圖	*Inducing Exercise Chart*
Dao Yin Lun	导引論	*On Inducing Qi*
Dong Heng Shi Shu	東恒拾書	*Ten Books of Dong Heng*
Du Fu	杜甫	Du Fu
Fang Hu Wai Shi	方壺外史	*Unofficial History of Fang Hu*
Gao Lian	高濂	Gao Lian
Ge Hong	葛洪	Ge Hong
Ge Zhi Yu Lun	格致余論	*Essay of Ge Zhi Yu*
Gong Ju Zhong	龔居中	Gong Ju Zhong
Gong Yan Xian	龔炎賢	Gong Yan Xian

PENYIN	CHINESE	ENGLISH
Guanzi	管子	Guanzi
Gui Zhong Zhi Nan	規中指南	*Guide to the Gui Zhong Point*
Guo Mo Ruo	郭沫若	Guo Mo Ruo
Han	漢	Han Dynasty
Hua Tuo	華佗	Hua Tuo
Hua Cun	華淳	Hua Cun
Huang Di Nei Jing	黄帝内經	*The Yellow Emperor's Classic of Internal Medicine*
Huang Ting Jing	黄庭經	*The Classic of the Yellow Court*
Huo Ren Xin Fa	活人心法	*The Inner Method of Preserving Life*
Ji Jing Ban Mai Kao	奇經百脉考	*Examination of the Eight Secondary Channels and Other Matters*
Jin Kui Yao Lue	金匱要略	*Brief Summary of Jin Kui*
Jing Zuo Gon Fu	靜坐功夫	*Silent Sitting*
Jiu Ceng Lian Xin	九層練心	*Nine Levels of Training The Heart*
Kang Zhuangzi	亢莊子	Kang Zhuangzi
Kongzi	孔子	Kongzi (Confucius)
Laozi	老子	Laozi (Lao Tsu)
Leng Qian	冷謙	Len Qian
Li Dong heng	李東恒	Li Dong heng
Li Bai	李白	Li Bai (Li Po)
Li Guo	李果	Li Guo
Li Han Xu	李寒虛	Li Han Xu
Li Shi Zhen	李時珍	Li Shi Zhen
Li Ting	李挺	Li Ting
Liu Yuan Su	劉元蘇	Liu Yuan Su
Lü Dong-Bin	呂洞賓	Lü Dong-Bing

PENYIN	CHINESE	ENGLISH
Lü Shi Chun Qiu Gu Yue Pian	吕氏春秋·古樂篇	The Spring and Autumn Annals, "Ancient Music"
Lun Heng	論恒	Essay on Balance
Lu Qian Yang	陸潛陽	Lu Qian Yang
Lu You	陸遊	Lu You
Mao Shan	茅山	Mao Shan division of Taoist School
Ma Wang Dui	馬王堆	Ma Wang Du Tomb
Mengzi	孟子	Mengzi (Mencius)
Qian Jin Fang	千金方	Essential Prescription Worth a Thousand in Gold
Qian Jin Yi Fang	千金翼方	Supplement to "Essential Prescription Worth a Thousand in Gold"
Qing	清	Qin Dynasty
Qu Bing Mi Jue	祛病秘訣	Secrets of Removing Pain
Quyuan	屈原	Quyuan
Qu Xian Ji	曲賢羈	Qi Xian Ji
Ru	儒	Confucian School
Ru Men Shi Qin	儒門事親	Self-Practice in the Confucian Tradition
Shang	商	Shang Dynasty
Shang Han Za Bin Lun	傷寒雜病	Essay on Disease Due to Cold and Other Miscellaneous Diseases
Shen Kuo	沈括	Shen Kuo
Shen Yin Shu	神隱書	The Book of Hidden Consciousness
Shi	釋	Buddhist School
Shi Shen Lun	攝生論	Essay on Preserving Life
Shou Shi Bao Yuan	寿世保元	Living a Long Life and Preserving Fundamental Energy
Sima Cheng-Zhen	司馬丞臻	Sima Cheng-Zhen
Si Ji Qu Bing Ge	四季祛病歌	Song of Curing Diseases During The Four Seasons

PENYIN	CHINESE	ENGLISH
Si Shi Tiao She	四時調攝	*Keeping Balance During The Four Seasons*
Su Shi	苏轼	Su Shi
Sun Simiao	孙思邈	Sun Simiao
Sun Zheng Ren Wei Shen Ge	孙真人	*Song For Eliminating Diseases in the Four Seasons By Sun Zheng Ren*
Tao Hongjing	陶弘景	Tao Hongjing
Tian Yin Shi Yang Shen Shu	天隐士養神書	*The Book of Keeping Fit By a Hermit*
Wai Tai Mi Yao	外臺秘要	*The Medical Secrets of an Official*
Wang An	王安	Wang An
Wang Chong	王充	Wang Chong
Wang Chong Yang	王重陽	Wang Chong Yang
Wang Shou	王寿	Wang Shou
Wei Boyang	魏伯陽	Wei Boyang
Wu Yao Yuan Quan	勿藥元筌	*The Great Book of Rehabilitation Without Using Medicine*
Wu Zheng Pian	悟真篇	*Understanding Truth*
Xia	夏	Xia Dynasty
Xia Ri	夏日	*Summer Time*
Xing Qi Yu Bei Ming	行氣玉佩銘	*The Inscription on the Jade Belt For Promoting Circulation*
Xiu Lin Yao Zhi	修靈要旨	*Principles of Practice*
Xu Ling Tai	徐靈臺	Xu Ling Tai
Xunzi	荀子	Xunzi
Yang Shen Dao Ying Tu	養神导引圖	*The Atlas of Physical, Breathing, and Health-Preserving Exercises*
Yang Shen Yan Ming Lu	養神延命錄	*How to Preserve Your Health and Extend Your Life Span*
Yanhui	顏回	Yanhui
Yan Nian Qu Bing Zhai	延年祛病摘	*Living a Long Life and How to Cure Disease*

PENYIN	CHINESE	ENGLISH
Yao and Shun	尧舜	Yao and Shun Period
Yi Xue Ru Men Bao Yang Shuo	醫學入門保養説	*Recuperation in Medical Science*
Yi Xue Yuan Lun	医學源論	*The Source of Medicine*
Yun Ji Qi Jian	雲笈七笈	*Seven Essays of Yun Ji*
Zhang Chong Zhen	張重珍	Zhang Chong Zhen
Zhang Jun Fang	張君房	Zhang Jun Fang
Zhang Zhong-Jing	張仲景	Zhang Zhong-Jing
Zhang Zi Yang	張紫陽	Zhang Zi Yang
Zhi Yi	智頤	Zhi Yi
Zhou	周	Zhou Dynasty
Zhuangzi	莊子	Zhuangzi (Chuang Tsu)
Zhu Bing Yuan Hou Lun	諸病源候論	*General Treatise on The Etiology and Symptomatology of Diseases*
Zhu Dan Xi	朱丹溪	Zhu Dan Xi
Zhu Zhen Xiang	朱臻翔	Zhu Zhen Xiang
Zuo Wang Lun	坐忘論	*On Sitting and Forgetting*

Glossary of Chinese Terms

PENYIN	CHINESE	ENGLISH
Bao	胞	Uterus, Ovary and Oviduct
Chong	冲	Chong Channel
Dantian	丹田	Literally: "Field of the Elixir." The term is used to refer to the area surrounding a point below the navel in which Qi is preserved and accessed. It is also used as a term for several other "fields" of energy: in the forehead (upper Dantian), breast, (middle Dantian), and lower abdomen (lower Dantian). The terminology varies over the course of the history of Qi Gong. In some texts, for instance, the lower abdominal Dantian is called the Middle Dantian, and the area above the Huiyin point is called the Lower Dantian.
Ding	定	Sitting and forgetting
Fu	腑	Fu organs: large intestine, small intestine, stomach, gall bladder, urinary bladder, tripple warmer. In General the Fu organs regulate digestion and the elimination of waste.
Guanyuan	関元	Acupuncture point: Ren, 4 meaning: The Guarding Gate
Huiyin	會陰	Acupuncture point: Ren, 1 meaning: gathering place of the Yin
Jing	精	Essence
Jing Qi Shen	精氣神	Essence, energy, spirit: The Three Treasures
Mingmen	命門	Acupuncture point: Du, 4 meaning: Gate of Life
Qi	氣	Psycho-physical energy
Qi Gong	氣功	Energy exercises

PENYIN	CHINESE	ENGLISH
Ru Jing	入靜	Practice of quieting the brain
Ren	任	Ren Channel
San Jiao	三焦	The Tripple Warmer
Shanzhong	膻中	Acupuncture point: Ren, 17
Shen	神	Spirit
Shenque	神闕	Middle Dantian
Xian	閑	Tranquility
Wei Qi	衛氣	Protecting Qi
Xin	心	Heart/mind
Xin	醒	Abstaining from meat or wine
Xing	形	Shape, posture
Yang	陽	The active aspect of energy
Yi	意	Mind, consciousness, intention
Yi Xing Qi	意形氣	Intention, Posture, Energy: The Three Regulations
Yin	陰	The receptive or yeilding aspect of energy
Yin / yang	陰陽	The active yielding aspects of energy taken together
Yongquan	涌泉	Accupuncture point: K, 1 meaning: Bubbling Well
Yuan Jing	元精	Congenital or primordial Jing (essence)
Yuan Qi	元氣	Congenital or primordial Qi (energy)
Yuan Shen	元神	Congenital or primordial Shen (spirit)

PENYIN	CHINESE	ENGLISH
Zang	臟	The Zang organs: heart, liver, spleen, kidney, lung. In general, the Zang organs regulate the generation, storage and distribution of energy.
Zang Fu	臟腑	The "Zang" and the "Fu" organs taken as a whole
Zang Fu Jing	臟腑經	Jing (essence) of the Zang Fu organs
Zheng Qi	正氣	Qi (energy) associated with the anti-pathogenic factor
Zhiguan	止觀	Looking within
Zhongji	中極	Acupuncture point: Ren, 3
Zhongwan	中脘	Acupuncture point: Ren, 12

Acknowledgements

Page 26: Caho Meng-fu, detail, *Twin Pines Against a Flat Vista*, The Metropolitan Museum of Art

Page 30: Wang Shing-min, *After Chu-jan's Snow Scene*, National Palace Museum, Taipei

Page 37: Zhu Gui, *Clearing Up After Spring Rain*, Selected Works of Jingling Artists, published by Oriental Culture Enterprises Co.

Page 38: Wang Hui, *After Chu-jan's Brushwork*, The Art Museum, Princeton University

Page 43: Fu Ershi, *Playing the Zither Along the Stream*, Selected Works of Jingling Artists, published by Oriental Culture Enterprises.

Page 78: Anonymous, *A Bridge Over A Stream Among Steep Mountains*, Liaoning Provincial Museum.

Page 86: Daoist Immortal; published: Suzuki Kei, comp., Chugoku kaiga sogo zuroku: daiikkan, Amerika-Kanada hen (Comprehensive illustrated catalogue of Chinese paintings: volume 1, American and Canadian Collections)(Tokyo: University of Tokyo Press, 1982).

Calligraphy for "List of Names and Titles" and "Glossary of Chinese Terms" by Yubo Wang

Other calligraphy by Tzu Kuo Shih